Social Anthropology

GODFREY LIENHARDT

Social Anthropology

Second Edition

OXFORD UNIVERSITY PRESS
London Oxford New York

Oxford University Press

OXFORD LONDON NEW YORK
GLASGOW TORONTO MELBOURNE WELLINGTON
CAPE TOWN SALISBURY IBADAN NAIROBI LUSAKA ADDIS ABABA
BOMBAY CALCUTTA MADRAS KARACHI LAHORE DACCA
KUALA LUMPUR SINGAPORE HONG KONG TOKYO

First published in the Home University Library *1964*
Second edition first published as an
Oxford University Press paperback 1966
This reprint 1969

PRINTED IN GREAT BRITAIN BY
HAZELL WATSON AND VINEY, LTD, AYLESBURY, BUCKS

To F. R. and Q. D. LEAVIS

_____

Contents

Preface

THIS book, in one form or another, has been in preparation for a long time. I was first asked to write it in 1956, and for several years before that A. R. Radcliffe-Brown, then Professor of Social Anthropology in Oxford, had been working on a draft which was left unfinished when he died in 1955. Most of what he had completed has since been published as *Method in Social Anthropology* (ed. M. N. Srinivas, 1958).

The first work on anthropology in the Home University Library, published in 1912 and still most instructive and readable, was that of Dr R. R. Marett, Rector of Exeter College, Oxford. Apart from his own intellectual contribution to the subject, especially in the field of religion, and the model of non-technical exposition he provided, Marett was a practical enthusiast, who did much to consolidate the subject in his own University and more widely. Following him half a century later, and also as a member of his college—still a home of anthropology in Oxford—I should like to pay tribute to his memory.

Social anthropology is a wide-ranging subject. As it has grown and changed since the time of Marett, it has tended, inevitably, towards a diversification of interests. To dwell on the specialized concerns of most anthropologists in their day-to-day work would not have been appropriate in an introduction of this kind, but I am conscious that some large and important subjects in social anthropology—linguistics, art, anthropological methods and techniques, for example—have been omitted. Others have been all too briefly mentioned, and some parts of

the world have been neglected. British anthropologists, naturally enough, are referred to more often than others who have
an equal claim to the serious reader's attention. I say this less by
way of apology (for this is not intended as a comprehensive
text-book) than to indicate that much is left for further study,
and I have tried to represent in the final book-list something of
what could not be included in the text.

Dewsbury, 1964   G. L.

Acknowledgements

I AM very grateful to the authors whose works I have quoted, and to their publishers. I thank the British Broadcasting Corporation and the Editor of the *Listener* for permission to reproduce at the end of Chapter 6 a very slightly modified form of a talk in a series called 'The Sacrificial Society', given on the Third Programme in 1960 and printed in the *Listener*, Vol. LXIV, No. 1632. The talk was conceived within the framework of this book, and to have put it into different words would have been a vain labour.

My colleagues at the Institute of Social Anthropology, Oxford University, have given me much assistance. Professor E. E. Evans-Pritchard, Dr J. H. M. Beattie, Dr D. F. Pocock, and Dr Peter Lienhardt have made valuable comments on most of the manuscript. Drs Rodney Needham, K. O. L. Burridge, and D. F. Pocock generously supplied written information on subjects in which they are specialists, and permitted me to use it at my discretion. Dr Ruth Finnegan (now Mrs Murray) made detailed criticisms and suggestions of a most helpful kind. I have discussed parts of the book also with Miss Wendy James and Mr Andrew Baring.

I have profited a great deal from the advice of non-anthropological friends. Mr D. M. Davin and Mr P. H. Sutcliffe gave just the kind of criticism, on literary and logical points throughout, which an author can best turn to advantage. Mr John Veale's remarks on the earlier chapters were similarly invaluable, and Dr T. P. Soper kindly commented, as an economist, on Chapter 4.

I thank also Mrs Davin, Mrs Hopkins, Miss Martha McCulloch, Karrar Ahmed Karrar, Mr Donald Stuart, Nana Nketsia IV, Mr Edwin Ardener, Mr P. Morton-Williams, Mr and Mrs John Metcalf, and my parents, all of whom contributed in their different ways to the completion of this book.

Note to the Second Impression of the Second Edition

I am grateful to Mrs R. Firth for suggesting corrections to the account of *kula* on pp. 83 and 84, which I have incorporated in this impression.

1
A Study of Man

There seems to be no human thought so primitive as to have lost
its bearing on our own thought, nor so ancient as to have broken its
connection with our own life.

E. B. Tylor, *Primitive Culture*

1

FOR THE MOST PART men live in society as in the physical
world, without reflecting on its nature. But as physical scientists
have gone beyond common experience in understanding the
physical universe, so social scientists have hoped for a deeper
and more systematic knowledge of societies than their members
themselves have or usually need in the day-to-day conduct of
affairs.

Social anthropology (under that name at least) is the youngest of the social sciences. It is connected with older and more
familiar subjects, particularly with history and sociology, and
cannot be neatly distinguished from them. But in general the
peoples who have been of greatest interest to social anthropologists have differed from those studied by historians on the
one hand or sociologists on the other in two principal ways.
They have lacked the written tradition that forms the subject
matter of history, or the kind of social and technological complexity of urban groups that has interested sociologists. They
are people whose societies traditionally (in E. E. Evans-
Pritchard's words) are 'small in scale with regard to numbers,
territory and range of social contacts, and which have by com-

parison with more advanced societies a simple technology and little specialization of social function'.

Social anthropologists have begun with the study of such 'primitive' societies, in the belief that the fundamental features of social institutions will be more apparent there than in modern metropolitan communities. They are in a position to study larger, more complicated societies too, and some have done so; but even then they start with a body of knowledge and theory gained from a training which puts the simpler, smaller non-industrial communities first. E. B. (Sir Edward) Tylor (1832–1917), in the early days of the subject, stressed the value of starting any examination of social institutions with a study of the small communities in which their essential features might be most readily discerned. The modern law student, for example, who 'plunges at once into the intricacies of legal systems which have grown up through the struggles, the reforms and even the blunders of thousands of years', might have been better prepared, Tylor thought, 'by seeing how laws begin in their simplest forms, framed to meet the needs of savage and barbaric tribes'.

Anthropology—of which social anthropology is a branch—began to become a distinct academic subject during the nineteenth century. In the background of the holistic study of Man which scholars then began to propose were the speculation and inquiries of generations of philosophers and travellers; and many familiar names, from Aristotle and Herodotus to Captain Cook and Locke, thus have a place in the history of anthropology.

This book is not intended to provide such a history, and even contributions made to the subject by modern professional writers may not always be attributed to them by name in the later chapters. The primary object is to give some account of what social anthropologists now know and think about the social life of 'exotic' societies, rather than to trace the growth of that knowledge.

But like other, more unambiguously 'scientific' subjects, social anthropology has developed by dismissing altogether some questions that once seemed to be of central importance, and restating others in the light of increased factual knowledge and understanding. So, for example, we no longer tax our ingenuity to provide likely accounts of the origins of any and every social institution—marriage, the family, religion, and so on. Since the theoretical interests and day-to-day preoccupations of modern students of the subject cannot be properly understood or evaluated without some awareness of this history of elimination and addition, we first sketch in the closer historical perspective.

Anthropological advances have often followed on the interests of governments in their own practical and moral problems. A famous case is that of the Ashanti of what is now Ghana, who went to war with their British rulers just over half a century ago. In 1900, the Governor of the Gold Coast asked the Ashanti why he was not invited to sit on the sacred Golden Stool of their nation, an act which, he thought, was necessary to confirm his sovereignty as Queen Victoria's representative. The ignorance and misunderstanding behind that demand led to war, for the Golden Stool had never been a throne. It was and is the shrine and symbol of the spirit of the Ashanti people. Further disorders might have followed, had not the Government seconded Captain Rattray—according to Edwin Smith's *The Golden Stool* (1927) 'a man of conspicuous ability and long experience, endowed with much tact and wholly sympathetic in his attitude towards the people'—to study the Ashanti and the place of the Golden Stool in their life. There followed a series of books by Rattray on many aspects of Ashanti culture, and a greater understanding between the Government and the people.

But many years before this, social anthropology (then called *ethnology* in England, as it still often is in France) was encouraged by the moral problems of the expanding European empires of the century. The nature and status of 'primitive' peoples, and the responsibilities of colonizers towards them, raised questions similar to those which had been asked, and answered in theological debate, by the Spanish rulers of the Indies some three hundred years before. First, were all the colonized peoples human as their colonizers were human?

A distinguished early anthropologist, James Cowles Prichard,

is an example of those Quakers and philanthropists of the early
nineteenth century who sought to use scientific knowledge of
different races in the interest of humane and just dealings with
them. In *The Natural History of Man* (1843) he set himself the
task of examining all available evidence about the physical and
moral characteristics of different peoples in order to find out
whether such an empirical study would confirm the teachings
of the Scriptures that 'it pleased the Almighty Creator to make
of one blood all the nations of the earth'. The question was not
simply academic or theological in implication as Prichard himself fully realized, for as he wrote:

If the Negro and Australian are not our fellow creatures and of one
family with ourselves but beings of an inferior order, and if our
duties towards them were not contemplated, as we may in that case
presume them not to have been, in any of the positive commands on
which the morality of the Christian world is founded, our relations
to these tribes will appear to be not very different from those which
might be imagined to subsist between us and a race of orangs.

Prichard's conclusions were those of all reputable students of
the subject: that purely scientific inquiry did support belief in a
basic unity of the human species, a similarity which outweighed
all conspicuous differences. All then were potentially comparable
socially and psychologically, as well as zoologically.

On the philanthropic and humanitarian side where Prichard's
interests were allied with those of such reformers as Buxton and
Hodgkin, the study of the condition of indigenous colonial
peoples led to the founding of the Aborigines' Protection
Society in 1837. This was also of great practical and scientific
importance for the growth of ethnology. As Prichard said,
thinking of the effects of European expansion, 'Many problems
of the most interesting and curious kind will have been left un-
solved if the various races of mankind become diminished in
number, and when the diversified tribes of America, Australia
and many parts of Asia shall have ceased to exist.'

This increasingly informed interest in very foreign peoples
was also catered for by the formation of learned societies. The
American Ethnological Society, the Ethnological Society of

Paris, and the Ethnological Society of London were all established in the early 1840's. The founders of the Ethnological Society of London issued a questionnaire on tribal custom, as a guide to travellers and officials who might contribute to the systematic study of Man everywhere, and also a journal, in which the contributions range from straightforward descriptions of foreign peoples and their countries to linguistic, historical, and biological studies and speculations. In this atmosphere of Christian humanitarianism and philanthropy, of colonialism, and of genuine scientific curiosity, the new study of Man developed in the earlier nineteenth century. To that time we trace the effective beginnings of the history of anthropology as an organized discipline more empirical, and in principle wider in scope, than the earlier philosophers' and historiographers' inquiries into the nature of human society.

The ethnologists of the last century were intent upon a universal history of mankind. They studied the physical characteristics of the different branches of the human species and their place within the animal kingdom; their geographical distribution; their spiritual and material cultures, and their conjectured historical relations with one another; and, at what now seems a very simple level, their social institutions. The study of physical types, under the name of Physical Anthropology, has since become a highly specialized and almost autonomous subject, allied more closely to anatomy, biology, and particularly genetics, than to social and cultural studies. The distribution of people, and of arts and customs, continues to be taught under the name of Ethnography, while the immense variety of men's cultural achievements and, as far as can be ascertained, their history, are the province of what now in England is called Ethnology.

Ethnology has tended to be identified with the study of material culture, and it is true that until the second decade of this century many of those in Britain who called themselves ethnologists tended to be more preoccupied with things than with people. But as K. O. L. Burridge has said,

behind the study of things lay the study of the people who made the things, living within the limits of particular environments and avail-

ing themselves of particular resources. These factors of specific environments, resources and historical circumstances, in relation to
the cultures and social institutions which have developed within
them, still form a basis for most social anthropological studies.

Social anthropology then is rooted in Ethnography and Ethnology which provided much of the information about human
societies analysed by 'armchair' anthropologists in the light of
sociological theory. But since the beginning of serious field-
research by social anthropologists in the early part of this century they have been able themselves to supply their own ethnographic and ethnological knowledge, and specialized ethnography and ethnology (unlike the physical anthropology and
prehistoric archaeology with which also they had close historic connexions), though taught separately in a few university courses, are only in practice distinct from social anthropology.

Around the middle of the nineteenth century, there began to
be proposed a managerial Science of Man, more ambitious than
had been contemplated by earlier ethnologists. This science,
which then began to be called 'anthropology', would aim at the
immediate discovery of universal 'laws' of human development
and human nature, as certain in their application as those of the
physical sciences. Once these laws were known, they were to be
used for regulating human affairs, particularly those of the non-
European peoples in their relations with European rulers.

Ironically, under the influence of such ambitions (more
cautiously and sympathetically expressed they have lived on in
some anthropological writings up to the present day), anthropology went through a period of extremely unscientific con-
troversy. In Britain, a leading exponent of this exact science of
human development was the contentious president of the newly
founded Anthropological Society of London, Dr James Hunt.
Hunt's dislike of the philanthropic bent of the older ethnologists was accompanied by wild racial prejudice, expressed, as it
often is, with pseudo-scientific detachment. Hunt maintained,
for example, that it was 'for the student of [anthropology] to
assign to each race the position it shall hold', and persuaded
himself and others that there were 'about six races below the

negro and six above him, taking the capacity of the cranium as a test'.

To begin to discuss this proposition nowadays would be like discussing Archbishop Ussher's reasons for asserting that the world was created in 4004 B.C. But its purpose was to justify the retention of negro slavery, through which the slaves, according to Hunt and his friends, were given opportunities to improve themselves by contact with a master race. Anthropologists and ethnologists now came more into the public eye (Hunt's Anthropological Society of London grew from eleven to five hundred members between 1863 and 1865), and became involved in heated disagreements with each other, with abolitionists, with missionaries, and with philanthropists—disagreements which were in origin political, theological, and moral rather than scientific. They did the subject small credit, and have little to do with any findings of modern anthropology, except as a warning. For they display in an obvious way the temptation (perhaps particularly in the social sciences) to give a seemingly scientific basis to attitudes and opinions not derived only, if at all, from dispassionate consideration of fact.

And from this point of view, Hunt's theory of a hierarchy of races (not without its appeal to more ignorant or equally tendentious people today) is of some interest. It exhibits very crudely a characteristic preoccupation of many later nineteenth-century anthropologists, a preoccupation that as we can now see came at least as much from circumstances of their own upbringing, and from their own social assumptions, as from their scientific inquiries. They were themselves reared in a strongly hierarchical society, taking for granted great and seemingly fixed distinctions of rank, wealth, and privilege; and in surveying the peoples of the world, they saw them also as hierarchically arranged, in a scheme of evolution or creation in which 'higher' and 'lower' races, higher and lower customs and beliefs, formed a gradation between the apelike and the godlike, or the infant and the adult, in Man. Wealth, and the technological and military superiority which went with it, seemed to confer moral precedence also. Living primitive peoples were regarded as analogous to the fossilized remains of those extinct organisms which formed part of the evidence for human physical evolution. They were thought to represent the earlier stages in a universal process of social evolution, on the whole progressive, which had gone furthest, it was thought, among the favoured Europeans.

The word 'evolution' is almost inseparable from the name of Charles Darwin, though theories of social evolution—of the stages by which men had made a transition from a state of nature to civilization—had been current long before his time. Darwin did however seem to demonstrate the way in which philosophical and historical speculation about human origins and development might be replaced by the beginnings of scientific certainty. His work thus encouraged the further application of an evolutionary philosophy to the study of social and moral differences between the peoples of the world. Tylor's book *Primitive Culture* (1871), pleased Darwin greatly.

It is wonderful [he wrote to Tylor] how you trace animism [belief in souls and spirits] from the lower races up to the religious belief of the highest races. . . . How curious also are the survivals or rudiments of old customs . . . I earnestly hope that you may be induced to treat morals in the same enlarged but careful manner . . . .

So it became a typical theoretical preoccupation of anthropologists of the century to arrange the peoples and social institutions of the world in an evolutionary series, from a theoretical primordial man to the civilized human being of mid-nineteenth-century Europe, 'from the ape to Annie Besant'. The uncritical procedures which this often involved produced a reaction against evolutionism, and even against history, among many social anthropologists of this century; and since living social anthropologists have been influenced by this reaction, we should consider briefly what 'evolutionary' anthropology was, and how it came to be discredited.

In Victorian times there were two main anthropological schools of thought about the general course of human history—a subject so vague and vast that no social anthropologist would be prepared to think it even meaningful today. Some students favoured a theory that human beings had on the whole progressively improved their minds and their social institutions. Darwin himself said that this was the 'truer and more cheerful view . . . that man had risen though by slow and interrupted steps, from a lowly condition to the highest standards yet attained by him in knowledge, morals and religion'.

It was taken for granted that Europeans of that time, and their social institutions, had attained those 'highest standards', and the self-complacency of some Victorians, offensive to the rest of mankind, has rightly been the butt of their grandchildren. Their optimistic theory of universal progress did however imply the possibility of *eventual* and potential equality between all the peoples of the earth, or at least between all those who showed themselves fit to survive. Those who were thought to be on the lower rungs of the ladder of human perfectibility were at least on the same ladder as their more advanced contemporaries. As had been seen, this was not accepted by all who called themselves anthropologists at the time, some of whom—Hunt already mentioned, his friend Captain (later Sir) Richard Burton, and the rationalist Winwood Reade among them—had strong views about the *natural* inferiority of the 'lower' races, and wished to justify on scientific-seeming grounds a permanent colonial rule.

The principal opponents of the philosophy of universal progress (for such it was, rather than a scientific theory) grounded their opinions partly in observation and partly in theological orthodoxy. Their most vocal representatives were Archbishop Whately of Dublin, and the Duke of Argyll, who held that the original condition of man had been 'higher' than that of many living primitive peoples of the time, some of whom must therefore have degenerated when driven into harsh environments, and now lacked the means or motive for independent self-improvement. Thus the letter of the Biblical and theological doctrine of Adam's original perfection might be preserved—a matter now neither here nor there for anthropology.

In the 'progressive' view of human social evolution, which was far more widely accepted among anthropological scholars, we now see clearly that European social standards of the period were being treated as definitive categories. This is explicit in the common use of the terms 'higher' and 'lower' races. Since it was taken for granted that the highest standards in knowledge, morals, and religion were at that time to be found among the educated classes of Europe and America, it was inferred that the converse of those standards must have been those of our earliest ancestors, of whom some living primitive tribes were thought to be the lingering survivals.

The 'higher' peoples were characterized by scientific reasoning and technological power, by strong 'representative' government and a developed sense of private property, by strict monogamy and an emphasis upon sexual morality, and by a religion of ethical monotheism. The 'lower' peoples therefore might be supposed to show the opposite of these characteristics—childlike thought-processes, uninventiveness, anarchy or tyranny in the political sphere, sexual and economic communism, and an amoral ritualism or total ignorance in religious matters. Even Charles Darwin, so exactingly observant as a naturalist, was able to persuade himself that he had seen peoples in this condition on his visit to Tierra del Fuego. After very superficial contact with them, he wrote:

The astonishment which I felt on first seeing a party of Fuegians on a wild and broken shore will never be forgotten by me, for the reflection at once rushed into my mind—such were our ancestors. These men were absolutely naked and bedaubed with paint, their long hair was tangled, their mouths frothed with excitement, and their expression wild, startled and distrustful. They possessed hardly any arts, and like wild animals lived on what they could catch; they had no government and were merciless to everyone not of their own small tribe.

And he went on to refer to 'the savage who delights to torture his enemies, offers up bloody sacrifices, practises infanticide without remorse, treats his wives like slaves, knows no decency and is haunted by the grossest superstitions'.

Such was one of the pictures of 'primitive man' which began to be built up around the middle of the nineteenth century. It was a picture less accurate, as we now know, than that accepted by humane ethnologists earlier in the century, and was the complete reverse of the romantic picture of 'the noble savage' of a still earlier period. (An interesting synthesis of ideals, that of the noble savage and that of the European gentleman, occurs later in the fiction of Edgar Rice Burroughs, whose noble savage, Tarzan, also turns out to be a British aristocrat.) Several influential writers—Herbert Spencer and Sir John Lubbock (Lord Avebury) among them—made what now seems to be a selective use of sources to show that living primitive peoples exhibited some or all of the 'lower' characteristics mentioned.

Theories were produced which even contemporary observations, had they been examined in a balanced way, could have been used to contradict. Darwin's account of the Fuegians, for example, first published in 1871, presents a very different picture from that of another visitor to Tierra del Fuego, W. P. Snow, who had already published an easily accessible description of the people in 1861 in the *Journal of the Ethnological Society of London*. According to Snow, the Fuegians were 'fine powerful looking fellows' though dirty and unkempt; their women were remarkable for their modesty; they were very fond of their children; some of their artifacts were ingenious; they recognized some sort of rights over property; and they accepted the authority of several of the oldest women. A later writer, E. Lucas Bridges, who lived for long with the Fuegians, has suggested in *Uttermost Part of the Earth* (1948) how they were first puzzled by the kind of interrogations to which they were subjected in Darwin's time, started to give the answers they thought were expected (to confirm the persistent suggestion that they were cannibals, for example), and finally made up fantastic stories for the amusement of seeing them taken seriously:

We are told that they described, with much detail, how the Fuegians ate their enemies killed in battle, and when there were no such victims, devoured their old women. When asked if they ate dogs when hungry, they said they did not, as dogs were useful for catching otter, where as old women were of no use at all.

It has been a major task of social anthropologists in this century to get at the truth behind such conflicting reports of travellers, by making their own observations at first hand; in doing so they have had to set aside much of the evolutionary dogma of the past. One classic example is enough to suggest how unhistorical and unscientific now appears the work of some scholars obsessed with comprehensive 'historical' reconstructions of social institutions. A most influential writer of the last century on the evolution of human society (Marx and Engels relied upon and probably popularized his work) was an American lawyer turned ethnologist, L. H. Morgan (1818–81). In *Ancient Society* (1877) he worked out a very elaborate *schema* of the whole course of human social development, from an original state of Savagery, through a condition he called Barbarism, to Civilization. He identified these stages by various material, technological, and institutional criteria, and attempted to fit all known societies, past and present, into the categories he proposed. Both in fact and in discrimination (for peoples of very different cultures were classified together) he was often wrong; but his work had the value of bold academic errors, in provoking reconsideration of the information, and in providing explicit theories which could be criticized by further reference to fact.

Before writing *Ancient Society*, Morgan had already attempted a large-scale reconstruction of the whole history of marriage and the family, *Systems of Consanguinity and Affinity of the Human Family* (1871), and still earlier had made one of the first scientific studies of American Indians, the *League of the Ho-de-no-saunee or Iroquois* (1851). His work on the family did elucidate certain principles of family structure unlike any known in Europe or America at the time, as will be seen in a later chapter. But not content with this, he set himself the task of trying to show that marriage and the family had developed or would develop universally through some fifteen defined stages, from an original state of total sexual promiscuity to civilized monogamous marriage. Earlier stages had survived, he asserted, among living primitive peoples of the time, and might further be inferred from ways of naming and addressing kin, very different from those of nineteenth-century Europeans, in various parts of the world.

According to Morgan, an original state of promiscuity had

given way to a form of group mating between brothers and sisters, producing what he called 'the communal family' as the first real family. He found some evidence for this in reports, from Hawaii and elsewhere, of current marriage customs (which almost certainly had been misunderstood) and of the terms used for describing and addressing relatives there. A Judge Andrews, for example, had reported that the Hawaiians had no separate words for 'uncle', 'aunt', 'nephew', 'niece'. All uncles and aunts were called by the same term as fathers and mothers; all nephews and nieces were called by the same term as brother and sister. From this, as Morgan thought, it might be concluded that brothers regularly had married their own sisters, in which case of course a man's father *would* also be his uncle and so on. We now know such an inference to be more than dubious; but in any case, it would not provide evidence for the contention that such a state of affairs at one time prevailed all over the world.

In the earlier forms of mating, a child would know its own mother, but not its father. Hence, Morgan thought (and here many of his contemporaries were in agreement with him), descent would be first counted through females, dividing people in matriarchal groups. The Iroquois did indeed trace descent through women. Promiscuity and group mating had then given way to individual mating, producing 'the barbarian family', which in turn had been succeeded by the marriage of one man to several women. This emphasized the importance of the senior male or patriarch, was accompanied by the tracing of descent through males, and produced 'the patriarchal family'. Finally, with the beginning of a conception of private property and the desire to transmit it to specific real heirs, came the civilized, monogamous family, for which Morgan had a warm reverence: 'the whole previous experience and progress of mankind culminated and crystallized in this one institution'.

Morgan's reconstruction of the development of the family is far more elaborate than this brief account suggests, and the elaboration only serves to expose more clearly the basic unsoundness of his procedure. Yet some of the evidence upon which it was based was at the time apparently convincing. There was indeed no evidence for the totally promiscuous stage, upon which all the others rest, but Morgan dismissed this difficulty by stating that evidence would certainly be found. It never has been. For the rest, there were reports of marriages between brothers and sisters (as in ancient Egypt) which would now appear to us as special ceremonial unions in some ruling houses; and there were accounts (largely based on misunderstandings) of the sharing of wives in something that might be taken for group-marriage. There was, and is, definite knowledge of peoples who take a number of wives; of people who for some purposes count their descent through women (though not usually because they do not know their fathers); and, of course, of monogamous marriage.

Morgan's fault, like that of many would-be historians of institutions at his time, was to try to arrange all these in a universal time sequence. We now accept that there is not and can never be any historical evidence for one original form of marriage or the family, or indeed that any one original form existed. Faced with such 'anthropological' theory as that of Morgan, historians might well be suspicious of anthropology and ethnology. As Maitland wrote:

When this evidence gets into the hands of men who have been trained in a severe school of history and who have been taught to look upon all social phenomena as interdependent it begins to prove far less than it used to prove. Each case begins to look very unique and a law which deduces that 'mother-right' (matriarchy) cannot come after 'father-right' (patriarchy) or which would establish any other similar sequence of 'states' begins to look exceedingly improbable. . . .

But such early evolutionary theories nevertheless made their contributions to the development of social anthropology. They sought order in a mass of confused information about human social life; and they continued over a wider range of knowledge, the attempt of the social philosophers of earlier vintage— Comte, ultimately, probably the greatest among them—to relate the institutions of many varied forms of society to one another, and to their own civilization. To arrange these diverse

social institutions in evolutionary sequence, it was at least necessary in some way to define, isolate, and compare them, and to
search for correlations between them.

Working on these lines while propounding evolutionary
theories of his own and somewhat different from those of
Morgan, J. F. McLennan (1827–81) began to examine and try
to explain the widespread custom of marrying outside the group
one is born into, a custom for which he coined the word 'exogamy' which is still in use. His explanation itself—that primitive tribes, finding their female children a burden, would prac-
tise female infanticide and hence have to seek their wives from
foreign groups—is a typical example of evolutionary imagination; but the rule of exogamy exists, and in trying to understand it McLennan furthered the study of marriage relations
between different tribes, clans, or lineages, while also establishing a connexion between exogamic marriage customs and
the religious phenomenon of totemism (the reverence for or
worship of different natural species identified, as 'totems', with
the solidarity of particular human groups, especially groups of
common ancestry).

So evolutionary studies, with all their confusions which it is
not profitable to dwell on in more detail, opened the way for a
comparative sociology that would not ignore less familiar tribal
institutions. The historian Seeley recognized that in neglecting
these, orthodox history had narrowed its understanding of
political affairs: 'When we have once got rid of the notion that
the tribes and clans of barbarism are contemptible and un-
worthy of attention, we obtain a somewhat different view of the
state,' he wrote.

And there were those ethnologists in the later nineteenth
century who had already begun to take a critical view of the
guesswork involved in attempts to reconstruct the social institutions of the earliest men. They had really started to under-
mine the evolutionary theories of their predecessors (even without being able themselves to escape from them) by trying to
draw a line between historical or ethnological knowledge and
mere plausible conjectures. Sir Henry Maine (1828–88) whose
legal training and classical studies combined with experience of

real affairs in India gave him a perspective that many others lacked, held that 'what mankind did in the primitive state may not be a hopeless subject of inquiry, but of their motives for doing it it is impossible to know anything'. For, he said,

The sketches of the plight of human beings in the first ages of the world are effected by first supposing mankind to be divested of a great part of the circumstances by which they are now surrounded, and then by assuming that, in the condition thus imagined, they would preserve the same sentiments and prejudices by which they are now actuated—although, in fact, these sentiments may have been created and engendered by the very circumstances of which, by hypothesis, they are to be stripped.

And Sir James Frazer (1854–1941), the author of *The Golden Bough*, a most significant work for introducing anthropology to a wider public, asserted in his inaugural lecture as the first professor to hold a chair of *social* anthropology (in 1908, at Liverpool) that the subject had 'nothing whatever to say about primitive man in the absolute sense'. It knew nothing, and never was likely to know anything, about him: 'To construct the history of human society by starting from absolutely primordial man and working down through thousands or millions of years to the institutions of existing savages might possibly have merit as a flight of imagination but it could have none as a work of science.'

Also by the beginning of this century, two requirements for the development of modern social anthropology had begun to be fulfilled. The first was the necessity for more careful, direct observation. No academic subject, clearly, could make progress when the very facts it proposed to interpret were represented quite differently by different observers, as with Darwin's and Snow's accounts of the people of Tierra del Fuego. The second requirement was for a more carefully considered and critical approach to the growing body of information about primitive society—for an approach which, like Maitland's 'severe school of history', would 'look upon all social phenomena as interdependent', and study them in their specific historical and geographical contexts.

2

There is a type of mind which cultivates the virtues of ethno-centricity, represents a distaste for foreigners as realistic and unsentimental common sense, and attributes to itself all the virtues of the civilization to which it belongs. It is a type of mind which will not open itself to the foreign experience which it yet judges with assured disdain, and which humane thinkers, many anthropologists among them, have for long had to contend with. Dr Johnson, for all his gifts, represents it:

Johnson: Now what a wretch must he be, who is content with such conversation as can be had among savages! You may remember an officer at Fort Augustus, who had served in America, told us of a woman they had to *bind* in order to get her back from savage life.
Boswell: She must have been an animal, a beast.
Johnson: Sir, she was a speaking cat.

Matthew Arnold was fighting against it in the 1860's, when in *The Function of Criticism at the Present Time* he questioned the 'exuberant self-satisfaction' of a speech by Sir Charles Adderley who had said:

Talk of the improvement of the breed! Why, the race we ourselves represent, the men and women, the old Anglo-Saxon race, are the best breed in the whole world . . . the absence of a too enervating climate, too unclouded skies and a too luxurious nature, has produced so vigorous a race of people, and rendered us so superior to the whole world.

So Aristotle had once thought of the Greeks, and examples of such arrogant judgements are numerous in later writings even up to the present day. They contribute to a climate of opinion in which even well-intentioned and moderately well-informed people may look with surprise on any practical attempt to approach a foreign people on their own terms.

Darwin's friend A. R. Wallace describes in his autobiography a dinner given by T. H. Huxley for the Russian ethnologist, Miklukho Maklay (1846–88), after whom the Ethnographic

Institute in Moscow is named. Maklay asserted that 'you could learn nothing about natives unless you lived with them and became almost one of themselves: above all, you must win their confidence and therefore begin by trusting them absolutely'. According to Wallace, Maklay himself had put this into practice to the point of remaining seated and smiling while tribesmen would 'draw their bows to the full with the arrow directed towards his chest, and then loose the string with a twang, while holding back the arrow'. This is an extreme example of self-accommodation to the ways of strangers; but at the other extremes were 'authorities' on primitive life who did not know even the elements of the languages of the people they described. Sir Francis Galton, who compared the Damara Hottentots' capacity for expressing themselves with that of his dog and suggested that they depended so much on signs that they could scarcely communicate at night, could have known nothing of their language.

Wallace and Huxley then were impressed by Maklay's ideas, and by his courage and success, for at that time the necessity of establishing human relations with indigenous peoples was not taken for granted even among travelled men. Wallace himself had been to New Guinea, but as a naturalist, like Darwin when he visited Tierra del Fuego. The study of the peoples of those distant parts was conducted casually at the side of more practical (and in the eyes of the world, important) research in biology, geography, and geology and zoology, or as a by-product of administration and missionary effort.

In America the situation was different from the beginning. The Indian populations lay within easier reach of scholars and the general public. They had not been easily subdued and therefore inspired some respect, while their treatment at the hands of their conquerors disturbed the consciences of many intelligent men; and they were intimately bound up with the whole of specifically American history. The problems they presented were thus nearer home to ordinary Americans than those raised for the British by the remote populations of the Empire.

Early official encouragement for ethnology and ethnography made for a very high standard of American field research in the nineteenth century. Under the auspices of the Bureau of Indian Affairs, Henry Schoolcraft began to publish (in 1853) his extensive work, *The Indian Tribes of North America*, parts of which read like the field notebooks of a competent modern social anthropologist and ethnographer. Schoolcraft had unusual personal advantages for his work among the Indians, for as he explains in his preface:

The peculiarly intimate relations the author has held to them (having married a highly educated lady, whose grandfather was a distinguished aboriginal chief-regnant or king), has had the effect of breaking down towards himself, individually, the eternal distrust and suspicion of the Indian mind.

In this tradition of direct observation are the numerous volumes published for the Bureau of Ethnology, an American foundation dating from 1879. The material which these publications contain is impressive indeed. The great body of native texts alone provides a solid literary basis for Amerindian studies—'Amerindian' is a convenient term for distinguishing the Indians of America from those of India—and the accounts of custom and culture published by the Bureau compare in thoroughness and quality of reporting with modern ethnographic studies. For example, the very first volume includes nearly 300 pages describing and illustrating the extensive sign language through which members of different tribes communicate with one another in an esperanto of gestures. Such orderly and detailed observations are far superior to most of the records of travellers and missionaries on which the anthropology of European possessions largely relied until this century.

A central figure in Amerindian studies was Franz Boas (1858–1942), who at one time or another taught many of the older generation of living American anthropologists. His expedition to study the Eskimos of Baffin Land in 1883-4, when he travelled by dog sled and with Eskimo companions, was one of the first attempts at field research undertaken for specifically anthropological ends. Though it was made while Boas was still a German citizen, and with financial help from a German newspaper, it was an introduction to the kind of work he was later to do after taking American nationality.

Boas's career shows something of the effect upon a serious scientific mind of direct contact with primitive cultures. According to his friend Ruth Benedict, his intention in going to the Eskimo had been to extend the geographical and environmental studies developed in Germany when he was a student. The harsh environment of the Eskimo might be supposed to provide an extreme example of the way in which physical environment (as Boas then supposed) was an ultimate determining factor in ways of life and thought.

In that first trip, discovering the range and complexity of cultural variation found within a fairly uniform environment, Boas saw that his early ideas of environmental determinism were quite inadequate. His interest turned to the complex interrelationship of detail in any single culture, and the connexions between the cultural and historical traditions of different peoples. Faced with the immense quantity of information which even the sparsest culture offers to a systematic ethnologist and which he was one of the first to collect in its fullness, and appreciating the intricate interdependencies of social and cultural facts, Boas also recognized the superficiality of earlier attempts to establish universal laws of cultural development: 'We must understand the process by which the individual culture grew,' he said, 'before we can undertake to lay down the laws by which the culture of all mankind grew.'

In turning from natural science (his doctorial thesis was on the colour of water) to ethnology, Boas changed also from the framework of thought of the natural sciences, primarily materialistic in the very nature of the phenomena, to that of history. For if (as he had found) the culture of the Eskimo was not to be reduced simply to material or physical causes, it could not be 'explained' only by ideas and procedures found appropriate for the study of the physical world. Those who envisaged 'a natural science of society', the British social anthropologist A. R. Radcliffe-Brown (1881–1955) prominent among them, placed the methodological emphasis differently. With Boas, they sought to discover the functional and structural interdependencies of social facts: but as many of the societies studied by social anthropologists have little recorded history, it seemed to Radcliffe-

Brown and others that explanations of features of the present life of those societies were to be sought less in a sequence of past events, than in the relationship between living social institutions.

And certainly the 'culture history' approach of a Boas has its limitations as well as its virtues. The kind of scholarship it encourages may become mere conjecture, if more cautious and learned conjecture than that of earlier scholars who attempted to re-create the history of human culture on a far larger scale. Some of the most stimulating influences in modern social anthropology have in fact come, not from those who saw the subject as a kind of history of culture (though this has its place) but from a scientific study of social relations irrespective, ultimately, of their particular cultural expression. So for the historian of cultures, ancient Roman family relations, let us say, are part of the social and cultural history of ancient Rome. For a social anthropologist also, they are this; but for him they may further be abstracted from the particular culture to which they belong, and compared with family relations among peoples of quite different cultural background. But such methodological discussion could scarcely have arisen without the first-hand experience of societies very different from their own sought by early field-workers, among whom Boas was outstanding.

Personal acquaintance with 'primitive' peoples also did something to minimize the supposed differences between 'primitive' and 'civilized' mentality upon which evolutionary theory had so heavily relied. Though certain psychological and physiological differences, like social differences, may well exist between different human groups, the study of them even now is not enough to warrant any generalized statement contrasting 'primitive' with 'civilized' man. Even the word 'primitive' as now used is merely a matter of literary convenience. Earlier writers were less cautious, and erroneous reports and misinterpretations led to false conclusions which only intensive research could begin to correct.

Boas's own work is here again to the point. In a course of lectures published under the title *The Mind of Primitive Man* (1913), Boas refers to a description of the mentality of the Indians of Vancouver Island given by G. M. Sproat in 1868: '. . . a short conversation wearies him [the Indian], particularly if questions are asked that require efforts of thought or memory on his part. The mind of the savage then appears to rock to and fro out of mere weakness.' The sociologist Herbert Spencer had offered this and similar reports as proof that primitive peoples were psychologically less evolved than civilized folk.

Boas put this observation to the test of his own experience of living with the very peoples whom Sproat had described. The Indian, he said, finds the traveller's questions trifling:

. . . he naturally soon tires of a conversation carried on in a foreign language, and one in which he finds nothing to interest him. As a matter of fact, the interest of those natives can easily be raised to a high pitch, and I have often been the one who was wearied out first.

And he turns to some of the characteristics for which the Indians of British Columbia have now become well known in anthropological literature:

Neither does the management of their intricate system of exchange prove mental inertness in matters which concern the natives. Without mnemonic aids, they plan the systematic distribution of their property in such a manner as to increase their wealth and social position. These plans require great foresight and constant application.

Boas in America, with his great influence as a teacher, thus heralded a change in the direction of his subject. In Britain, a decisive sign of a similar change appeared in 1898, when the well-equipped Cambridge Expedition to the Torres Straits landed on Thursday Island in Melanesia. This expedition was led by A. C. Haddon (a zoologist become ethnologist and ethnographer and the founder of anthropological teaching in Cambridge) and included medical doctors, experimental psychologists, a trained linguist, and a recorder of music. At that time, there was no specialized *social* anthropology; Haddon and the others, especially W. H. R. Rivers, one of the psychologists and later well known as an ethnologist, collected such information as came to hand. The several volumes of reports of the expedition attempt to produce a far fuller account of Melanesian people in all aspects of their life than had previously been attempted for any peoples of British territories.

One contribution particularly has had a lasting influence in social anthropology—the use by Rivers of what was called 'the genealogical method' of investigation. A physician by training, Rivers was interested in the study of hereditary aptitudes and disabilities, and it was in order to explore this question that he began to collect genealogies. The sociological value of recording the genealogical relationships of individuals, especially in societies where the range and strength of ties of kindred tend to be far greater than in metropolitan conditions, is now taken for granted in anthropological research. But at that time even Rivers himself did not fully recognize the variety of information that could be acquired by understanding in detail the relationships he had started to record. From the point of view of modern anthropology it is curious to read his admission that when he was in Murray Island he 'did not inquire whether there were any special functions connected with ties of kinship'. It was only later that he grasped how far the collection of genealogies in their full complication would help to provide one important key to the understanding of social organization, when he had begun to see that the difference between real and adoptive parentage was socially very significant (it had created great confusion for those trying to administer the law) and that not all those who appeared as close kin on genealogies were actually biologically so.

Expeditions of whole teams of investigators are more expensive than anthropological funds have commonly permitted. Fortunately, research conducted by teams of specialists is not the only source of sound anthropological knowledge, nor has it always proved the best. The very presence of a *group* of foreign investigators tends to modify the relations that any one of them can establish with the people among whom they are living, and what they gain in breadth of field may sometimes be lost in depth. The success of the Torres Straits Expedition has been attributed by more than one writer to the strong personality of A. C. Haddon himself, with his genuine interest in the Melanesians as human beings (he was concerned by the effect of European exploitation of them) as well as his anxiety to tap a source of scientific knowledge then fast drying up.

Hence, much of the most able field-research in social anthropology has been carried out not by teams of scholars, but by individuals isolated, like Miklukho Maklay or Boas earlier, among the people they wished to study. Modern theory has depended primarily upon the accumulation of these detailed individual studies of particular peoples made in the light of a comparative knowledge of many societies acquired by technical training or reading.

Some of the conclusions that may be drawn from this body of detailed information will appear in later chapters. The knowledge itself began to be collected with ever-increasing detail in the first decades of this century. To name only a few examples, Edward Westermarck went to Morocco (1900), Rivers to the Todas of South India (1901–2) and Melanesia (1908, 1914), A. R. Radcliffe-Brown to the Andaman Islands (1906), C. G. and B. Z. Seligman to the Sudan (1909), R. Thurnwald to Melanesia (1906–9), G. Lindblom to the Akamba of East Africa (1910), and Malinowski, probably the most famous of European field anthropologists of the time, lived with the Trobriand Islanders, as an alternative to internment elsewhere, during the 1914–18 war. All these went out to make intensive professional studies, and produced accounts of their research which are still recommended anthropological reading.

Thorough and experienced *non*-professional observers of primitive peoples, to whom social anthropology owes a great deal, are still more numerous from the later nineteenth century onwards. Only a few need be mentioned. A valuable early monograph is Callaway's *The Religious System of the Amazulu* (1870), probably the first annotated collection of African texts. R. H. Codrington, a missionary, wrote his work *The Melanesians* (1891). The Dutch Islamic scholar Snouck Hurgronje produced his study of the Achehenese of Sumatra (1893, in English 1906), an example of anthropology in the service of administration. H. Junod, a Swiss missionary, was working on his excellent *The Life of a South African Tribe* (translated 1912–13), and

Spencer and Gillen were beginning to publish their rich material on the Australian aborigines. In America, the collection of information about the Amerindians continued as enthusiastically as before. The body of specialized and sound information upon which social anthropologists now rely was thus beginning to grow very quickly.

Some students of ethnology and ethnography have remained content simply to gather and contemplate interesting facts about exotic peoples in a spirit of dedicated antiquarianism. But as in other disciplines, the stimulus for research has been produced by those others, intellectually more exacting, who seek unifying principles or theories, in the light of which whole ranges of facts may be seen to be interrelated in a coherent way. So the fault of the evolutionary anthropologists previously mentioned was not indeed that they propounded theories, but that the theories were based on very inadequate information and, in so far as they involved a great deal of guesswork about primordial man, could never be tested. They were thus philosophical dogmas rather than scientific theories.

In the earlier days of anthropology, the qualities in a student that make for the collection of good information, and those that make for its unification and synthesis, were not usually found in the same person. In Europe it was not until the second decade or so of this century, with Malinowski, particularly, that intensive field-work was combined with a desire or ability to produce generalizations which (whether they have proved sound or not) have the virtue of encouraging others to test them by further examination of the facts. Boas in America certainly combined field research with generalization; but he tended to divide the two, and cannot be said to have produced ideas which still provoke methodological argument.

It has been in the course of disagreements on points of fact and interpretation that social anthropology has established certain generally acceptable, if modest, theoretical principles. Many of the interests of modern students of the subject began to be defined and clarified earlier in the century in a kind of dialogue, between those—whether anthropologists or not— who had the opportunity of observing primitive peoples directly, and those who at home collected, classified, and inter-preted this diverse information. Such scholars, 'armchair an-thropologists' as they are often called, played an important part in building up the discipline, and it is sometimes regretted that today there are not more of them, to give direction to the sep-arate labours of hosts of field anthropologists.

In England Tylor himself had done much to present anthro-pology to the public as a unified study of Man which would lighten the burden of learning by reducing the complexities of cultures and societies to a relatively few simple principles. In some directions, he had enunciated such principles himself, for example in coining the word 'animism' for the basic religious beliefs of primitive peoples, and giving as its minimal definition 'a belief in spiritual beings'. This definition is not of much help to us today, but in its time it did at least establish that the mat-erial objects—carved figures, trees and rocks, 'magic' bundles and so on—in which primitive divinities are often located or figured, were not worshipped as material forms, but as repre-sentations of spiritual realities. The investigation of primitive religion which has now gone so much further could have made little progress had this simple conclusion not been drawn from early writings on the subject.

The foremost of British 'armchair' anthropologists, Sir James Frazer, became for many years the interpreter of religious and magical beliefs to a public far wider than that of professional anthropologists, as may be judged from allusions to his work in the poetry of T. S. Eliot, or the enthusiasm of Ezra Pound: 'As Voltaire was a needed light in the eighteenth century, so in our time Frazer and Fabre have been essentials in the mental furnishings of any mind qualified to write of ethics, philosophy or that mixed molasses, religion.' In addition to his own wide reading—*The Golden Bough* is of value as an encyclopaedia and bibliography alone—Frazer had an extensive range of admiring correspondents in foreign parts who were able to make in-quiries on the spot about customs and beliefs which he drew to their attention. He produced a questionnaire for their general guidance, and gave them much personal encouragement in their researches on his behalf. His then was a type of the unifying and speculating mind that has had an important role in creating some sort of order out of the ever-accumulating mass of detail with which anthropologists must always be faced.

It is true that Frazer's broad general idea of the universal scheme of psychological evolution, from magical thought to religious belief, from religious belief to scientific thought, has not proved in itself to be of any great value. Magical, religious, and scientific ways of understanding the world have been shown to coexist, though at different levels of individual and communal experience. Tylor was disturbed by the growth even in Europe of spiritualism among educated and otherwise 'scientific' people in his time, and the scientist A. R. Wallace records how he himself recommended a spirit-medium whom he had found 'entirely trustworthy' to the poet Tennyson. On the other hand, among primitive peoples, as Malinowski was later to emphasize, magical and religious practices are by no means the whole of life. Technical skill and rational calculation are exhibited by all in practical daily affairs, and in earlier writings on primitive society 'the proportion of knowledge to credulity is greatly underestimated', as Elsie Clews Parsons observed.

Frazer's psychological insight, on which he prided himself, was often at fault, largely because he thought that he could understand very foreign beliefs quite out of their real contexts simply by an effort of introspection. He and others of his time had something of the approach of Sherlock Holmes in the works of his near-contemporary, Conan Doyle: 'You know my methods in such cases, Watson: I put myself in the man's place, and having first gauged his intelligence, I try to imagine how I myself should have proceeded under the same circumstances.' Such deductive procedures might have their merits in the study of people with whom the investigator had much in common. They could only mislead where the student was a middle-class Victorian scholar, and the subject an Australian aborigine or ancient Egyptian priest. Nevertheless Frazer's was a remarkable achievement. He showed the possibility of a wide-ranging comparative study of religion, which would reveal underlying similarities between 'advanced' and 'savage' beliefs; and he did begin to identify and define certain widespread institutions, notably that of 'divine kingship' where the king is also high priest, still frequently referred to by anthropologists.

He also made some effort to explain the function of institutions or beliefs which, in themselves, might appear merely foolish or repulsive to the average book-educated European of his day. His essays in *Psyche's Task* attempt to show (by what seemed to him a paradox) that 'superstitions' had often been useful in upholding respect for government, private property, marriage, and human life. In other words, such erroneous beliefs had performed the functions of supporting institutions which, from Frazer's point of view, were of central importance for any social order.

This notion of exhibiting the positive social *functions* of unfamiliar customs and beliefs, developed almost over-systematically by writers like Radcliffe-Brown and Malinowski, has had an intellectually vital influence on modern social anthropology. It may be seen, for example, in M. Gluckman's *Custom and Conflict in Africa* (1955). It would be unprofitable here to discuss the methodological arguments (some of them, as it now appears, sadly sterile) involved in what came to be labelled the 'functionalist' approach. It may be accepted, though, that this approach, which assumes that any society can be studied as an organic whole of which the parts are functionally interdependent, finally divided our primarily *social* anthropology from the broad 'culture history' of earlier anthropologists and ethnologists. For the latter, to 'explain' a custom or belief had been to investigate its history and search for its supposed origin, either in time, or in some universal psychological characteristics of Man. The explanation of the constitution of any society thus lay either in the past, or in human psychology. Students of social function on the other hand sought the explanation primarily in the present—in the existing relations between the different institutions of any society.

For, as Radcliffe-Brown pointed out, to explain how an institution came into existence is not necessarily to explain how it continues in existence at the present day. So, for example, a study of the history of the English monarchy simply as a chronological sequence of events causally connected with each other would not in itself be enough to account for the position of the monarchy in our modern society. For this, we should have to show the relations between the monarchy and some, at least, of our other living social institutions—Parliament, the Established Church, the modern Press and so on. To go further in understanding, we might then compare those relations of the present time with the relations between the monarchy and other social institutions in the past. Such would have been the view of a greater 'armchair' anthropologist than Sir James Frazer, a more systematic thinker, and one to whom the subject owes more of its current ideas—the French sociologist Emile Durkheim (1858–1917).

Emile Durkheim, with his colleagues Mauss, Hubert, and others, proposed towards the end of the nineteenth century a more subtly considered 'science of society' than earlier exponents of social science on the grand scale—Herbert Spencer or even Comte himself—had achieved. In the *Année Sociologique*, where many of their contributions to social anthropology are to be found, Durkheim made clear in the first issue one of the principles upon which an autonomous and scholarly social science might in his views be based. He wanted to see (as some social anthropologists want to see today) a closer understanding between historians and sociologists; and he wanted to remove from their studies some of the merely *a priori* philosophical and psychological assumptions of earlier writers.

Durkheim had himself been a pupil of Fustel de Coulanges, some of whose work—especially *The Ancient City* (1864), a study of early Italian society—is still read today. But Durkheim envisaged a sociology which (unlike purely historical work) would place the institutions of ancient literate societies studied by historians and classical scholars in a wider context of living primitive custom and belief. He suggested, for example, that Fustel de Coulanges would have been in a better position to understand what the Romans meant by *sacer*, 'sacred', had he been able to view it in the light of anthropological findings about the nature of sacredness in other parts of the world—in relation to the Polynesian idea of *taboo* in particular. For as

Durkheim said '. . . it is only possible to explain by making comparisons. Without this, even simple description is scarcely possible; one can scarcely describe a single fact, or one of which there are only rare examples, *because one cannot see it well enough*' (my italics). If historians in Durkheim's view tended to show a too exclusive interest in the particularities and details of their small chosen fields of study, sociologists were rightly suspect in the eyes of historians for 'the too general nature of (their) theories and their insufficient documentation'.

Durkheim's theoretical treatise, *The Rules of Sociological Method*, first published in France in 1894, still stands as a landmark in the often dreary wastes of writings on sociological 'methodology', a subject in which he was deeply interested. As the American sociologist Talcott Parsons observes, Durkheim 'never theorized in the air' but was always seeking the solution of important empirical problems. An example is his work *Suicide* (1897). Though naturally it does not measure up to modern standards of sociological inquiry it is a systematic attempt to correlate the incidence of suicide with other social factors. In *The Rules of Sociological Method* he established several principles of investigation which, by and large, his successors have found it profitable to observe. Among them is his insistence that since social life is not the product of any individual's psychology, it cannot be adequately understood by reference to the consciousness and motivation of individuals only.

Tylor and others had tried to 'explain' some aspects of primitive religion by suggesting that primitive individuals had as it were *reasoned* with themselves about such common phenomena as dreams and apparitions, and had thereby arrived at a conception of the human soul. They had then, it was supposed, extended this idea from the human individual to the world at large, thus forming eventually a notion of a great spirit—God. Such interpretations seemed to Durkheim wrong-headed, for they could neither be empirically tested, nor would they account for the organization, and the varied organizations of religious beliefs. Such account as could, at the best, be given of the individual reactions and states of mind of participants in a religious ceremony would even then not tell us much about the nature of the church to which they belonged, and its relation to other social institutions.

To be sure, as Durkheim fully admitted, a society ultimately consists of the interrelated individuals who compose and have composed it, and nothing more. But, to use his own analogy, a society is something other than a collection of individuals, as 'the fluidity of water, its alimentary and other properties, are not in the two gases of which it is composed, but in the complex substance they form by their association'. If taken too literally (as some sociological methodologists have taken their analogies between societies and physical substances, machines or biological organisms) this could readily be shown to be misleading, but taken merely as a simile of the relation between individuals and the society of which they are members, it has some illustrative value. Something *is* involved in the social interaction of individuals that is not to be found wholly in any one of them, as is obvious in 'mob psychology', in the fact that a crowd will behave as none, or few, of the individuals it comprises would behave individually. Le Bon's *The Crowd* (trs. 1896) and Trotter's once widely read *Instincts of the Herd in Peace and War* (1916) are early examinations of this distinction.

In Durkheim's own writing, particularly in *The Elementary Forms of the Religious Life* (1912), some less obvious implications of this interaction and integration of the individual with the collective are examined. We shall return to some of them later. In general, the French sociologists of Durkheim's school established convincingly that social tradition moulds the individual conscience more fully than even the most self-conscious members of a society usually recognize. Different societies exhibit different *patterns* of thought, different 'collective representations' as the French called them, and these collective representations are the object of specifically sociological study. Anyone reflecting upon himself, and trying to take a detached view of his own reaction to custom—either of his own society, or of another —may come to recognize that, without as it were rationally choosing them, he has taken over many habits of thought and evaluation from the social milieu in which he has grown up, and that there is nothing *intrinsically* stranger in the custom of one people than in that of another, any more than an elephant is intrinsically stranger than a horse. Such was Durkheim's view, and such was Seeley's: 'compare the most advanced state with the most primitive tribe, and you will see the same features, though the proportions are different'.

Social anthropology has become a study of such differences in proportion, aiming finally perhaps—in Durkheim's own words —'to reach the scientific facts under the level of the unscientific'. The reader will judge from the following chapters how, and how far, such a comparative knowledge of traditional societies as we now have can lead towards this end.

2
People and Environments

No bears have come because there is no ice, and there is no ice
because there is no wind, and there is no wind because we have
offended the powers....

An Eskimo

EVEN THE SIMPLEST DESCRIPTION of a foreign society
would obviously be incomplete without discussion of its geographical location and natural environment, and if only for this
reason social anthropologists have to begin with geographical
and topographical knowledge. But further, social relations are
influenced by environment and all the more subtly and directly
for peoples with little technological control over nature who
must adapt themselves immediately to its demands. A year of
late rains, ruining the harvest and bringing famine, may mean
the dispersal of a whole community to live scattered among
more fortunate kin and neighbours or throw themselves on the
mercy of foreigners. Such changes affect many social relationships. Hence most modern anthropological studies are grounded in a systematic examination of the interrelations of human
communities with their environments—in human ecology.

Human ecology begins with commonsense observations on
the relations between nature and men, and then develops them
further and in fuller detail. Clearly their particular mode of life
in the desert makes some of the Arabian Bedouin dependent
upon the camel, but only detailed investigation will demonstrate
how this dependence and all that it implies is connected with
the political relations between specific Bedouin tribes.

Again, among some of the cattle-herding Nilotic Africans of the Southern Sudan, the herds must be taken to pastures near the main rivers in the dry season, for there is then neither water nor grass elsewhere. The necessity for this general movement is apparent from the regional circumstances. Less obviously, in some Nilotic areas the incidence of tribal fighting can be correlated from year to year with readings from river gauges situated far from the pastures in which the fighting occurs. The authors of *The Equatorial Nile Project* (a report for the Sudan Government on possibilities of controlling some of the Nile waters) found that in some places 'High levels in the dry season spell trouble and a definite deterioration of public security.' The rate of discharge of the Nile shown at Mongalla, for example, may indicate whether or not tribal fighting is likely in pastures many miles to the north. The explanation of this is ecological, as will be seen when the ecology of this area is more fully discussed later in the chapter (see p. 39).

Among many peoples—the Bedouin and the Eskimo are two very different examples—the intractable environment sets strict limits to possible modes of existence. Such peoples have little choice as to their general way of life. But even among them (as Boas and others found) physical factors do not absolutely determine the details of culture. C. Daryll Forde's comparative study of many quite dissimilar societies in relation to their geographic environments, *Habitat, Economy and Society* (1934), ends by confirming the view of Lucien Fèbvre: 'Between the desires and needs of man, and everything in nature that can be utilized by him, beliefs, ideas and customs interpose . . . we are never concerned with "man", but with human society and its organized groups.'

In other words, for the sort of understanding of people and environments needed in social anthropology, it is not enough to produce a full geographic account of the environment as the fixed scenery standing as a background to the cultural activities of its inhabitants. What is of interest is the nature of the adaptation of people to environment in any given region, and this is what ecological study tries to demonstrate. In such an investigation, old-fashioned arguments between those who regarded the environment as dominating men, and those who drew attention to the plasticity and freedom of the human will and imagination, become irrelevant. What we have to ask is how far environmental necessity in any particular area can be used as an adequate explanation of human behaviour, and at what points other, intrinsically sociological, explanations become more reasonable.

In the statement by an Eskimo which heads this chapter, the central question if of course 'Why are there no bears?'—an important question for the Eskimo whose material well-being is at stake. His answer shows a knowledge of the habits of bears and their relation to environmental conditions. It is an observation on animal ecology, and is of anthropological interest in showing that the Eskimo entertain perfectly rational explanations of events. But there is nothing in the Eskimo environment that makes the last stage of the argument—'and there is no wind because we have offended the powers'—inevitable. Here the Eskimo moves from rational observation to an interpretation which is essentially part of a human cultural tradition. And it is here that a social anthropologist, who is interested in the behaviour of bears not for its own sake but for its effects on human thought and behaviour, may begin his real work.

The Eskimo were in fact among the first people to provoke detailed inquiries into the relation between sociological and ecological factors in tribal life. Marcel Mauss, probably the most notable of Durkheim's colleagues and certainly his equal, published in the *Année Sociologique* for 1905 a study of the social organization of the Eskimo interpreted in relation to their environment and economy, his 'Essai sur les variations saisonnières des sociétés Eskimo'. The subtitle of this essay, 'a study in social morphology', indicates something of what Mauss and his colleagues wished to achieve. As in biology 'morphology' involves the study of the forms of organisms, and in philology the study of the forms of words, so in sociology there might be a specialized investigation into the forms of human association, a social morphology.

Behind this there lay a broader set of theoretical principles accepted by the writers of the *Année Sociologique*, and already touched upon earlier (Chap. 1, pp. 29–31). They had the idea, more cogent in its detailed application than may appear when it is briefly summarized, that when members of a social group are in close and intense contact, they manifest moral characteristics and generate kinds of behaviour different from those found among the same individuals when they are isolated and dispersed.

According to this theory our experience of the sustaining value of society is itself the source of religious conceptions and behaviour. In worshipping the gods, men are in fact admitting and confirming their awareness of the protective and formative powers of their societies which, like the gods, impose upon them particular codes of behaviour and punish infraction of those codes. Society itself then is the source of conceptions of the divine—'the sacred'—and sacredness is attributed to those objects, activities, and relationships which are essential for social existence. 'Profane' and secular affairs on the other hand are those which concern individuals as such, or the smaller component groups of the whole society. Hence, as with the distinction between the individual and the communal interest, there is in every society a distinction between the domain of 'the sacred' and the domain of 'the profane'. To study the former is to establish the characteristics of a *collective* life, distinguishable from the characteristics of its component individual lives, and the special subject matter of any strictly sociological investigation. The question these sociologists were asking themselves then was 'what is the nature and what are the forms of social integration?'

From reading about the Eskimo (for he was no field-worker) it seemed to Mauss that they offered a good opportunity for putting such theories to the test in a specific ethnographic context. Despite ecological differences between different groups, one bold environmental factor deeply affects them all: the yearly contrast in these polar regions between winter and summer conditions. In winter, the rivers, lakes, and creeks, and much of the sea itself, are icebound. In summer, the ice and snow melt, baring the ground for the growth of stunted vegetation and freeing the waterways. The melting of the ice, of course, makes communications more, not less, difficult. The American technicians in Eskimoland at the present day still have to cope with this situation, for it is only while the waters are frozen that they can be easily crossed and used as landing strips.

In these circumstances, many of the Eskimo have had to change their mode of life with the seasons. In winter, seal and walrus are accessible to Eskimo methods of hunting—methods which depend upon an extremely elaborate, ingenious, and specialized technology. In summer—especially among the Central Eskimo—the natural harvest is inland. Land animals, the most important among them the caribou, are hunted, and various kinds of artic plant life are collected for food.

Therefore in their quest for food and for the natural materials from which they have constructed their very complex material culture, the Eskimo have to live near the sea and its inlets in winter, and disperse over the inland territories in summer. In winter, they live in concentrated communities, in houses made either of stone or of snow, near the frozen waters. In summer, they separate into smaller groups, and move inland to hunt and collect wild fruits, living in skin tents and shelters.

This very general outline of Eskimo ecology suggests why they provided a good testing-ground for Mauss's sociological theory of the special qualities and characteristics of social aggregation. Here was a society which for clearly demonstrable environmental reasons had in every year a period of social concentration, and a period of more individual wandering and dispersal. In his essay, Mauss urged that these two periods in the round of the Eskimo year were associated with two quite different, if complementary, kinds of social relations:

. . . the people have two ways of grouping themselves, and to these two ways of grouping correspond two juridical systems, two moral systems, two sorts of domestic economy and of religious life. To a real community of ideas and interests in the dense agglomerations of the winter, with a strong moral and religious unity, are opposed an isolation, a social atomization, and an extreme moral and religious poverty in the dispersal of the summer.

There would be something very satisfying in the demonstration of such co-ordinations between moral and physical solidarity, if the evidence really did point to it without question. But Mauss went too far in stressing a complete antithesis between the 'moral life' of the Eskimo in the summer and in the winter. It is after all the very same Eskimo who seasonally gather together and disperse, and in their relatively small and isolated groups of the summer they still belong also to the larger groupings of the winter. It is not then really a matter of two quite different types of society at the two different seasons. There is one set of religious beliefs, social institutions, and so on, but emphasized and expressed differently according to the season.

Nevertheless, the main principle of Mauss's analysis of Eskimo society stands—that is, that the periods of aggregation are also the periods of the greatest social and religious activity, and of the most complex interrelations of individuals and families. The demonstrable link between the Eskimo and their environment does affect social relations, and in ways which may be accurately ascertained.

There could scarcely be a greater contrast between environments, peoples, and modes of life than that between the small, mongoloid, and thickly clad Eskimo of the Arctic, and the tall, lightly clad or naked Nilotic negroes of the swampy basin of the Nile in the Southern Sudan. Neither a geographer nor, probably, a professional ecologist, might think at first sight that a comparison between them served much purpose for their sciences. But there is one ecological point of resemblance between these peoples which is of sociological interest.

The Nilotics whose ecology has been most fully related to sociological analysis of their political institutions are the Nuer, some 400,000 people divided into several tribes, living partly by horticulture but with an overriding interest in their large herds of cattle. The herds not only supply many of their material needs. Cattle are given in exchange for brides and used for sacrifice, and thus have a moral as well as an economic importance.

Nuerland is a vast plain around central papyrus swamps,

crossed by rivers and watercourses flowing towards the main streams of the Nile. Here again, there is a very sharp contrast between summer and winter conditions. Summer (say from June to November) is a season of rains and floods, winter (or more precisely winter and early spring, from December to April) a season of rainless months and ultimately complete drought.

In summer, the rivers and streams overflow their banks and water covers the country, except for scattered mounds and ridges which alone are then habitable. On these elevated places, Nuer build permanent villages and cultivate during the rains. Both men and cattle are then distributed over the country in relatively small and isolated communities.

After floods have subsided and during the dry winter, grass and water for the herds become scarce near many of the villages. The higher sites soon dry out and there is grazing only near the banks and confluences of rivers. Nuer village communities which have been dispersed and isolated for the wet summer are therefore compelled to gather together in a few favourable areas by the main rivers in each tribal territory. It is in this connexion that the readings of a river gauge in one place may be correlated with political events in another many miles away; in certain measurable conditions of flooding or of low water more people than some pastures will actually provide for may be forced to share them. The more restricted the grazing, the greater the competition for it, and the greater therefore the likelihood of hostilities.

The social importance of Nuer movement—technically 'transhumance'—between separate summer villages, and concentrated winter camps on the banks of rivers is not difficult to understand. People who are effectively independent of each other at one season of the year are brought into close contact at another. Consequently unless there is to be constant strife, members of different villages must recognize a kind of rule of law between them for part of the year. The size of their political communities is affected in any place (for conditions differ from one area to another) by the extent and nature of their transhumance.

Also—a matter more fully discussed in the next chapter—the building up and breaking down of political communities every year is connected with the extremely decentralized form of political system found among the Nuer. The villagers who are autonomous during the isolation of the rains do not surrender this autonomy when they form larger groups during the drought. They accept certain conventions in their political relations with each other, but they accept rule from nobody.

So the Nuer and Eskimo, culturally and socially very different in almost all other respects, are comparable in the effect of ecological circumstances upon social relations. When the separate and autonomous groups of a tribe concentrate together in response to the pressure of the season—the icebound winter of the Eskimo, the dry winter of the Nuer—there must be some means of maintaining a degree of peace between them. In the effects of their ecology on political facts, the Nuer are indeed more like the Eskimo than like their neighbours and kinsmen the Anuak, whose agricultural way of life and environment in combination enable each little village community to be self-sufficient for the whole of the year. The largest political community of the Anuak is the village itself or confederation of villages and not, as with the Nuer, a large number of scattered villages combining in a much bigger unit, a tribe.

In one respect the information about the Nuer enables us to question some of Mauss's conclusions about the Eskimo. The main sacrificial and ceremonial season of the Nuer does *not* occur at the time when they are in their largest aggregations, at the height of the dry season, but just after the harvest, when the rains have more or less ceased but people are still living in their separate villages. Thus Mauss's analysis of the relation between concentration of total population and religious activity does not hold for the Nuer, at least if mere physical concentration is in question. His more general demonstration of the significance of ecological factors for social relations still stands, and it has been part of the work of social anthropologists since Mauss's time to examine their significance in particular local circumstances.

These references to Eskimo and Nuer have suggested something of the way in which ecology is connected with political and religious life. But the main and most obvious effect of environment on a primitive people is of course upon their economy—on how they gain a livelihood—and it is through the economy that environment most influences social relations. If, as for the Bedouin, the environment favours camel-herding, and if looking after camels in those conditions demands the co-operation of members of more than one family, that wider co-operation is to some extent the result of environment and economy. For the Bushmen of the Kalahari, on the other hand, the food supply is scanty and widely dispersed, and large groupings could not survive in any small area. The environment, combined with the mode of economic life, here favours very small groups.

For the anthropological discussion of economy and ecology, it is convenient to have a broad classification of the principal means by which peoples gain their livelihood; and here some permanent contribution was made by the evolutionary thinkers of the last century. Their classification divided the non-industrial societies into three main groups distinguished by their basic economic pursuits. First, there were the collectors of wild harvests and hunters (hunters and collectors as they are called) neither practising agriculture nor keeping domestic animals. Such peoples are the Pygmies and the Bushmen of Africa, some of the Australian aborigines, and the Penan of central Borneo and other small Indonesian groups. Second, there were the numerous pastoral peoples of the world; and third, the settled agricultural peoples.

In accordance with the evolutionary preconceptions of the time, these three basic types of economy were thought of as three stages in the universal history of Man: hunting and collecting peoples had eventually domesticated animals and thus 'progressed' towards a pastoral way of life, and thence towards agriculture and the settled peasant cultures from which rose the civilizations of antiquity. There is archaeological evidence in places for such changes over long periods of prehistory; but there is little or no evidence that any of the tribal peoples known to Europe in the nineteenth century would independently have evolved in this way. Often indeed environmental conditions would clearly prohibit such a change.

A more ambitious attempt to correlate types of economy with social differences of other kinds was made by Hobhouse, Wheeler, and Ginsberg in their *The Material Culture and Social Institutions of the Simpler Peoples* (1915); and, though their work would have been more securely based had they been able to use the information on ecology and on social life that has been collected since their time, their conclusions are still of some interest.

They introduced refinements into the simple threefold classification of hunters and collectors, herders, and agricultural people. For example, they divided the hunting peoples into Lower and Higher Hunters. Their Lower Hunters were such peoples as the Bushmen and Pygmies, without permanent dwellings, pottery, or indigenous metalwork, while the Higher Hunters were represented by the Indians of British Columbia, or the Plains Indians of America. These, though relying largely upon a wild harvest (of fish, and buffalo, respectively), had far more certain and extensive food supplies, and were materially far richer. Another subclass of hunters, Dependent Hunters, were certain peoples found chiefly in Malaya and India, whose hunting and collecting economy was closely linked to settled villages, where the hunters from time to time could exchange their surplus produce and sometimes sell their labour.

The authors of this book were working within a framework of evolutionary assumptions, as the very use of the terms 'lower' and 'higher' suggests, but even so they contradicted some of the more optimistic beliefs in universal material and moral progress of their predecessors. (Here the date of publication— 1915—during the disillusionment of the Great War, may be significant.) Writing of the connexion between technology and social organization, Hobhouse and his collaborators observed that on the whole the variations between more and less technologically complex societies accorded with general probability:

... for the economic development may be taken as a rough index of the amount of intellect and organizing power available for the shaping of the life of a society. Accordingly, we are prepared to find that in points indicative of social organization, there is a certain correspondence with economic advance. This we have found in the development of government and of justice alike, and in the fact that as we mount the scale there is more of government and more of the public administration of justice within society, and in the fact that the unit for government and justice extends.

Here, a modern social anthropologist would make it clear that it is not to differences in the material culture or technology of peoples alone that differences in the scale of societies—from small Pygmy bands to large African kingdoms even in the same regions—should be referred. There are intrinsically social factors which we shall later consider; but also, the ecological situation is obviously important. It is clear that the 'unit for government' among some of the hunting and collecting peoples *must* be small, because their mode of gaining a livelihood in their particular environment demands wide seasonal dispersal. Extensive government organization is neither feasible, nor necessary. On the other hand, where, as among the Amerindians of British Columbia, the wild harvest is plentiful, assured, and concentrated, it will feed larger settled communities. There we should expect what we find—a more complex form of social organization, with greater differences of power, rank, and wealth. Among ourselves the ordering of social relations in a family, or other small group whose members are in regular personal contact, is similarly of a different kind from that necessary in larger social units.

But as the Hobhouse, Wheeler, and Ginsberg survey points out, economic development '. . . has no necessary connection with improvement in the relations between members of a society. It does not imply greater considerateness or a keener sense of justice, and may in some ways be held to be adverse to them . . . .'' This is a view which would have startled some of the Victorians—Sir Samuel Baker, for example, with his conviction that 'The philanthropist and the missionary will expend their noble energies in vain against the obtuseness of savage hordes, until the first steps towards their enlightenment shall have been made by commerce . . . .' It is a view also which might be considered by those who do not wish to be disappointed by the social results of economic planning.

Such studies have helped to clarify the sorts of questions we can reasonably ask about the relation between material, and moral and intellectual, factors in social life; and ecologists have sometimes ended with as much respect for primitive peoples' ingenious adaptations to difficult environments as for the modern technological power which at first sight seems to make such ingenuity unnecessary. So an agronomist, P. de Schlippe, concerned with an elaborate government scheme for developing a more Western type of economy among the Azande people of the Sudan, was led to contrast the facts of Zande ecology with the visions of their improvement seen by technicians:

On one side there is the curriculum of Cambridge . . . with, in the background, a field of uniform golden wheat falling under the blades of a McCormick combine-harvester. On the other side there is the extraordinarily intricate fabric of a traditional system of agriculture on the background of a mottled pattern of grass-bush land which a small hoe and a small axe, helped by fire, transform into a no less mottled pattern of crops, varieties and associations.

Where the adaptation to environment is so intricate and delicate, to disturb it may have unforeseen effects. An interesting example is that of the Plains Indians of America who, before the introduction of the horse by the Spaniards, were not able to exist without a certain amount of steady agriculture. With the horse, they were able to neglect their agriculture and exist as hunters; but when Europeans (also an ecological factor) ploughed up the prairies, and almost exterminated the herds of buffalo upon which these Indians had now become almost entirely dependent, their lot became 'more pathetic than that of other less specialized Indian cultures', as Frazer Darling has said. The horse, which the Indians received from foreigners and used towards fuller domination of their environment, was one of a set of ecological factors which in the long run weakened Indian culture. But again, that culture would have been ill adapted to the political and business life of modern America. Had their relationship with the physical environment remained unchanged, their adaptation to the wider political and social environment could not have developed even to the limited extent it has.

Here in the study of human ecology there is a link with the study of history, and moral considerations enter which are not involved in the study of the ecological adaptation of plants or animals. The failure of many now extinct non-human organisms to change with their environmental circumstances could not properly be described as 'pathetic', for those lower organisms could not have become rationally aware of the complex influences exerted upon them. In studying as systematically as possible the relation between environment and human life, the human ecologist proposes an understanding of the possibilities and results of human acts, and it is for this reason that some students of the subject have concerned themselves with the moral as well as the physical side of adaptation. A large American symposium, *Man's Role in Changing the Face of the Earth* (from which the Eskimo's statement which heads this chapter is taken), shows much evidence of this concern. A traditional African village, for example, is there compared with a regimented settlement for African mineworkers in the Congo, not only as showing two sorts of relationships between men and nature, but also as indicating differences in the quality of social life, and ultimately, in philosophy: 'The workers and their families living in these cells are uprooted and depersonalized beings. . . . They are estranged from nature and each other.'

Whether or not this conclusion follows strictly from ecological studies, such moral assessments have a part in them today. With modern means of exploitation of environment, many ecological problems are not of adaptation to a 'natural' environment, but to an environment which men themselves have made, and in some cases, made difficult to live in. So when a pastoral people, with the resources of veterinary science, are able to keep more cattle than their land will support, overgrazing and erosion present them with other difficulties in place of those caused by plagues and parasites. Particularly for a social anthropologist, it is not the reasons for or nature of environmental influences in themselves which are of primary

interest, but the social effects of those influences. If it be once
established, as we are told, that 'the reindeer population of
Alaska crashed from 65,000 to 25,000 in about ten years', the
botanical, zoological, or climatological reasons for that fact are
not really significant sociologically. For whatever the reasons
(unless they are the acts of other human groups, and therefore
affect relations between peoples) the social effects will be much
the same.

There is a further dimension to the study of peoples and their
environments, and again one which particularly concerns social
anthropologists, as distinct from ecologists or geographers.
Men's adaptation to their environment greatly influences not
only material culture but also systems of ideas—symbolism,
principles of classification, the apprehension of time, space, and
direction and so on. Symbolism, imagery, and metaphor in any
language cannot but derive largely from men's reaction to their
environment and understanding of their place in it. In English
poetry, for example, an English reader will receive immediately
from a phrase an impression that for those not familiar with
the natural setting could only be produced by lengthy description. Take for example 'winter':

> Now is the winter of our discontent
> Made glorious summer by this sun of York ...

This imagery would contradict Eskimo experience, for their
winter is associated with contentment and feasting, summer
with wandering and separation. Again, the image of black or
lowering clouds, usually foreboding or depressing to the English town-dweller, is hopeful and joyous for many peoples who
anxiously watch the sky for the seasonal rains upon which their
pastures and agriculture depend.

Nor is it only knowledge of the natural setting in itself which
will give the necessary key to a people's imagery. Their own
relation to it—their ecology, in fact—is what must be known.
In *The Andaman Islanders* (1922) A. R. Radcliffe-Brown was one
of the first to work out in detail the connexion between religious and mythological beliefs, and the particular local ecological circumstances as necessary for an understanding of them.

The exposition is intricate but one example will give some indication of its nature.

The Andaman Islanders, a hunting, collecting, and fishing people off the coast of Burma in the Bay of Bengal, have a god, or legendary hero, called *Biliku*, who is associated with (among other things) violent seasonal winds and storms which, occurring in one part of the year, are taken to be signs of his anger. One of their beliefs about *Biliku* is that he is angry when beeswax is melted and burnt, that is, when honey is plentiful, which in turn is at the time of year bringing violent storms. How does Radcliffe-Brown account for this association of a god, winds, and the burning of beeswax? He writes:

... honey belongs particularly to the *Biliku* portion of the year .... As the natives make use of the wax, and as this is useless until it has been melted, this is the special season of the melting of bees' wax. At the beginning of the season the *Biliku* wind blows calmly .... As the season draws to a close the wind becomes variable, uncertain, and in some years violent storms occur ushering in the rains of the S.W. monsoons. Year after year, the wax-melting season comes to a close in stormy weather.

This ecological commentary will not of course 'explain' the whole of Andamanese religion; but without it, we could no more begin to understand the Andaman association between a god, a season, winds, anger, and beeswax, than we could understand 'the winter of our discontent' without knowing what 'winter' meant to an Elizabethan English community.

In many ways also human experience of living in particular environments influences such apparently abstract conceptions as those of time, space, and classification. It is a familiar experience to find time passing slowly or quickly, or for a given distance travelled to seem further in adverse conditions than in comfortable circumstances. This experience, however, for ourselves, assumes a set of abstract measurements of time and space—so many miles, so many hours—which are accepted as representing 'real' time and distance.

Among many peoples such abstract measurements are not used, or would be irrelevant to the effective rhythms of life. It is this in part which has resulted in common European generalizations that 'primitive' peoples 'have no sense of time', or cannot explain accurately how far it is from one place to another to guide a foreign traveller. But for people whose activities are not co-ordinated by clocks time seems to have a different quality. A particular date established by the calendar is not in itself significant for those who await the rains in order to start cultivation. What is important is the event itself—the coming of the rains, the growth of the crops, the period of the harvest; notions of time, therefore, are derived partly from such sequences of significant events. As E. E. Evans-Pritchard has written of the Nuer: '. . . they cannot . . . as we can, speak of time as though it were something actual, which passes, can be wasted, can be saved, and so forth. . . . Events follow a logical order, but they are not controlled by an abstract system.' Consequently, as with many peoples who are free from clocks and calendars, the Nuer take their bearings in time from what they are actually doing. It is such and such a period of the year because they are building dams for fishing, moving to dry-season camps, or whatever it may be that the natural rhythm imposes. They name and count lunar months, but they count them less certainly in the dry season, when social life is uneventful, than in the wet, when more is happening. It is thus not uncommon among African peoples for two of the months or 'moons' of the dry season to be called by the same name, for there is no special reason to distinguish them. And in farming communities everywhere, human tasks are co-ordinated in relation to natural conditions which do not vary with exact dates or times of day. Abstract measurements of time are hence less significant for them than for townsmen, who have to organize their complex activities without reference to the changes in the natural world.

As with time, so with space. Abstractly calculated distances between communities may be less significant than the social evaluation of those distances. The members of a pastoral group are more effectively separated from neighbouring agricultural peoples in *social* space, as it has been called, than from their own pastoral kinsmen who may live much further away, while a 'distant' relative (in social space) may be physically next door. As is shown by the communications between desert or sea-faring Arabs, great tracts of desert or expanses of sea do not necessarily create social division to the same extent as less conspicuous differences between adjoining geographical zones, offering different possibilities for human exploitation. Nor is it simply a matter of different environment. Residents on the coast of Kent, for example, are socially nearer to London than to Calais. This is not merely because in this case the sea is a greater obstacle to regular communications than the land. Here other factors, historical, political, and sociological, enter into the evaluation of distance, and it is here that a social anthropologist, having taken full account of environmental influences and adaptations in human thought and behaviour, begins to consider intrinsically sociological explanations for them.

3
Political Life

The incessant bickering and contests between encroaching chief
and jealous kinsmen; the weak central power; the divided
jurisdictions; the obstinacy with which a man of high birth insists
on the proper punctilio to be reciprocated between himself and his
Chief—all these are tokens of a free society in the rough....

Sir Alfred Lyall, Asiatic Studies

FROM THE BEGINNING of the *Politics*, Aristotle asserts that
the State is a natural institution, since it is in the very nature of
men to draw together for friendship and protection. Hobbes
(with a very different kind of State in mind) represents an opposed view. The State for him was an 'artificial man', an inven-
tion necessary for promoting the common good of mutually
hostile, self-centred, and competitive individuals: 'men have no
pleasure, but on the contrary a great deal of grief, in keeping
company, where there is no power able to over-awe them all'.

Political theory has influenced observers of political life
among peoples very different from those known to Aristotle or
to Hobbes. Where there was no conspicuous government, there
often seemed to be intolerable confusion and disorder, while
the roles and authority of indigenous rulers were often misunderstood, or, if understood, deplored. In the essay contain-
ing the passage quoted at the head of this chapter, Sir Alfred
Lyall was reflecting on the virtues of the 'natural', original
political systems of Rajputana in relation to British administrative policies there. He adds:

To make haste to help the Chief break the power of his turbulent and reactionary nobles, in order that he may establish police and uniform administration over his whole territory, is to an Englishman at first sight an obvious duty, at the second looks a dubious and short-sighted policy.

It was a policy owing more to Hobbes than to Aristotle.

Sociological investigators as well as men of affairs may be influenced more than they recognize by philosophical and psychological theories of the nature of men and the state. Those whose tendency it is to emphasize human self-interest and individualism seek to explain how it is possible for political associations to hold together at all, and draw more attention therefore to the formal and coercive aspects of political control than those who see political co-operation as a natural consequence of man's gregariousness.

Social anthropologists in the last thirty years or so at least have tried to examine empirically the nature of political combinations, disregarding the theoretical possibilities and merits or demerits of types of régime, and aiming to discover what actually are the principles regulating the internal and external relations of members of different political communities. And here societies which have grown and flourished without any appearance of formal government are at least as instructive as the familiar monarchies, aristocracies, oligarchies, and republics. The study of these 'tribes without rulers' as they are called in the title of a recent symposium on them (*Tribes without Rulers*, ed. Middleton and Tait, 1958) directs attention to basic principles of political action and combination rather than to the more familiar forms of constituted governments; and anthropological studies have probably made their most distinctive contribution to political science in showing how politics are conducted amongst peoples not subject to a central authority. For, as is clear in international politics, communities are able to maintain regular political relations without any single power 'able to over-awe them all'.

Contrary to what has often been supposed, there seems to be no society in which the sole principle of political combination is blood relationship between all its members. In *Government and Politics in Tribal Societies* (1956) I. Schapera has shown that even the small wandering bands of the Bushmen lay claim to distinct territories, and thus recognize the bond of a common homeland, even though most members of the band may also be close relatives or affines. An early survey of writings on the aborigines of Australia, *The Tribe, and Intertribal Relations in Australia* (G. C. Wheeler, 1910), similarly concludes that their small bands had clearly demarcated territorial boundaries:

... many of the ideas of International Law [were] clearly developed— territorial sovereignty, the sacredness of messengers and envoys, a normal and recognized intercourse over wide areas through inter- marriage and the exchange of commodities, and the existence in many cases of the rights of asylum, domicilement and hospitality.

Nevertheless the hunting and collecting peoples in general, living in the small groups their way of life necessitates, are so united by kinship, marriage, and frequent individual contact that it is difficult among them to separate political from domes- tic affairs.

But in many much larger societies, as has long been recog- nized, political loyalties are often spoken of in the idiom of kin- ship. Gibbon's account of the Tartars in the twenty-sixth chap- ter of his history of the Roman Empire here anticipates the more detailed understanding of the present day in a passage ad- mirable for its economy and simplicity:

The tribes of Scythia, distinguished by the modern appellation of Hords, assume the form of a numerous and increasing family; which, in the course of successive generations, has been propagated from the same original stock. The meanest, and most ignorant, of the Tartars, preserve, with conscious pride, the inestimable treasure of their genealogy; and whatever distinction of rank may have been introduced, by the unequal distribution of pastoral wealth, they mutually respect themselves, and each other, as the descendants of the first founder of the tribe. The custom, which still prevails, of adopting the bravest, and most faithful, of the captives, may coun- tenance the very probable suspicion, that this extensive consanguin- ity is, in great measure, legal and fictitious.

So very large populations may explain their political composition by reference to ancestry and descent. The powerful 'Aneza Bedouin tribes of Arabia, comprising some twenty thousand tents and owning more than a million camels, may still be represented on a single genealogical chart, as may the 800,000 Tiv of Nigeria.

The 'kinship' between different sections of such large nations cannot have exactly the same meaning for them as their kinship with an inmediate circle of close relatives. For the analysis of political relations it is therefore necessary to distinguish kinship and affinity as principles of social aggregation and co-operation, from the tracing of distant common ancestry. These in turn can be distinguished from other principles: that of co-residence in a common territory, and that of incorporation into specialized associations. It is convenient, though it involves a slight digression, to consider these in reverse order.

Associations of very various kinds incorporate individuals who share particular common qualities or interests. Churches, armies, guilds, clubs, and special societies existing to promote the interests and influence of their members are all different kinds of associations. Some associations—certain churches and armies are obvious examples—recruit their membership irrespective of nationality, country, kinship affiliations, or heredity. Some, such as guilds of craftsmen, recruit on the basis of occupation. Some recruit on the basis of age, like the age-sets and age-regiments of many East African peoples, in which all those initiated as adults at about the same time are united by that bond, and share a common name and common interests throughout their lives. Kinship affiliations and descent may also be a basis of membership, as when among the Ashanti of Ghana, who for most purposes count descent through the mother's side of the family, young men become members of their fathers' military companies. Membership of associations then may be conferred by membership of groups of different kinds; but in general it has no *necessary* connexion with the other three principles of aggregation. Though the age-sets of the East Africans, for example, incorporate generations of men of a particular tribe or section of a tribe into well-defined social groups, the local members of an age-set know its equivalents in neighbouring territories. Regimental organization based upon age-sets may stretch far beyond the boundaries of tribal territory, providing a basis for political unity where no other exists, as among the Nandi-speakers of Kenya.

Secret or semi-secret societies very typical of parts of West Africa, also in some places politically influential, again may spread quite beyond the confines of local groups, as the Poro society spreads over the frontiers of modern West African states. Associations may also be formed to further the interests of those who are united by loyalties of other kinds, as when tribes and peoples form co-operatives for their tribal economic benefit— Kilimanjaro Native Co-operative Union in Tanganyika is a case in point—and there are primarily political associations created to promote specifically nationalist ends. In general it is characteristic of associations that persons are not born into them, though birth, nationality, or other factors may provide the qualifications for membership.

Associations in great number and variety are particularly characteristic social groupings in modern states, where some, like the Trades Unions, are of considerable political significance. The territorial principle of political combination is similarly very familiar in world politics today. A 'state', both in common usage and in anthropological writings, is composed of the inhabitants of a specific territorial area along with those subject to the jurisdiction of the government of that area, even though they may not be permanently domiciled within it. And this is perhaps more particularly so for British readers, for as Namier pointed out, their concepts of nationality (along with those of the Swiss) are essentially territorial:

Indeed, the English language lacks a word to describe a 'nationality' distinct from, or contrasted with, the citizenship derived from territory and State; and the meaningless term of 'race' is often used for what in Continental languages is covered by 'nationality'.

The idea of a state, then, involves the notions of a territory with acknowledged boundaries, and of a government for the administration of that territory. When anthropologists use the word 'state', they also have in mind a polity in which some form of central government, or at least permanent leadership, is effective throughout a defined territorial area. The editors of *African Political Systems* (1940) classified certain African polities as 'state-like' or centralized, as contrasted with tribes without rulers on the one side, or small bands of persons united by kinship and affinity on the other.

But as has been said, even the small bands of the Bushmen or the Australian aborigines also exploit and defend a common territory and may be called by the name of that territory. There is thus some territorial basis for political unity everywhere, though it has not always been such a predominant factor in determining political loyalties as in the modern nation-state. With many peoples, the other two principles of political combination —that of kinship and affinity, and that of descent—play a much greater part.

The proper name of a family or descent group may be derived from the name of the place it comes from—the House of Windsor, for example. Conversely, an important family or group may give its own proper name to the whole place or territory it lives in. Then whole mixed communities of peoples of different ancestry may be known by a single name which originally belonged only to one group among them. Working through unfamiliar languages, anthropologists did not always find it easy, therefore, to distinguish between communities and social groups actually claiming common ancestry, and those united by sharing a common territory, for both kinds of groupings might be known by the same vernacular name.

The common and necessary words 'clan' and 'tribe' can be sources of confusion of this sort. Earlier anthropologists, and non-anthropologists today, tend to call any subdivision of a 'primitive' society a 'clan', and what are really villages, or political sections of other kinds, thus sometimes go under this name in past writings. In modern anthropological analysis the term 'clan' refers exclusively to descent groups composed of all those people who ultimately trace their origin to the same ancestor or ancestress. Descent from the clan-founder may be traced through males only or through women only. In the first case we speak of patrilineal clans, in the second of matrilineal. There are also various ways in which clan-membership is conferred by taking into account both paternal and maternal clan affiliations.

How widely the individual members of any particular clan may be living dispersed throughout the whole tribal territory varies from one people to another. Even among the same people some clans may be more and some less localized, like English surnames. The anthropologists' main interest is in the nature and distribution of corporate local groups of clansmen and their inter-relations. In some societies these local corporate groups are small, little more than large families. Then a clansman's knowledge of his line of descent may extend to only two or three generations from the present, and after that there is no pretence at certain knowledge of the further genealogical links to the clan-founder; so clansmen from different areas simply infer that they must be of the same clan because they share the same name and traditional observances.

Where clanship is politically more significant, a fuller genealogical knowledge is claimed, and living groups of clansmen claim to know with some certainty the genealogical links between themselves and the founding ancestor. Here the clan has a systematic genealogical structure, with numerous branches, now always called 'lineages' though in older writings the word 'sept' may be used. These lineages stand in known genealogical relationships to one another.

'Tribe', like 'clan', has been used both for groups united by descent, and for groups united by territorial allegiance. Often, as with the 'tribes' of Israel, these two principles of social integration are combined: but in such cases it is important to recognize that every single person who belongs politically to a 'tribe' is not necessarily descended from the supposed founder of that tribe, as Gibbon recognized in writing that the 'extensive consanguinity' of the Tartar tribes was probably in large measure 'legal and fictitious'. In most anthropological writings now, 'tribe' is used to mean a major political and territorial division of a larger, loosely organized cultural and ethnic group, a people or nation. Many tribes are subdivided into smaller more or less autonomous political sections.

Tribes and their sections then are political communities composed of groups of people of different lines of ancestry occupying a common territory. Clans and their lineages are descent groups of people claiming common ancestry whose individual members often are territorially widely scattered. In some cases clans may have only their knowledge of originating in the same clan-founder in common. There are tribes which, like those of the Nuer, include groups of clansmen from many quite different clans, and where strict rules against marrying within one's own lineage or clan ensure that alliances with unrelated people are constantly being formed. One clan from the many represented may then be recognized as having priority in the whole tribal territory, and those living within that territory who are not members of that clan will explain their presence by their relationship to those who are. The lineages or branches of a 'dominant' clan of this type spread throughout all the territorial sections of the tribe, and others who live in these sections identify themselves politically with their own lineage of the dominant clan even though they do not belong to it by descent.

Among some peoples a higher proportion of the members may claim to be agnatically related, however distantly, and the tribe—the political community—is represented as a single genealogical structure and thus has the *form* of a clan. This is the case with the Nigerian Tiv and 'Aneza Bedouin already mentioned, and many others. But everywhere there is some recognition of the difference between the kinship of individuals through a recent common ancestor living a few generations ago, and political 'kinship' between much larger groups who express their connexions with one another in terms of the relationship between distant figures—often mere names—in a tribal genealogy.

There is good practical and theoretical reason therefore for distinguishing the little descent group of a father or grandfather and his children, which is really no more than the nucleus of a large family, from clans and lineages, whose members trace their relationship much further into the past. A lineage of, say, five generations in depth, may have several hundred members, and thus constitute a large, effective political group. The descendants of a common great-grand-father necessarily form a group with different and smaller potentialities, though united on formally similar principles.

The genealogical tree of a clan or tribe is thus a guide to the political loyalties of its members and their place in society. The Somali say that what a person's address is in Europe, his genealogy is in Somaliland. A man helps those who are more nearly related to him in the genealogy against those who are more distant, until, in theory at least, the whole clan or tribe is united against all others. The descendants of a common great-grandfather are united on occasions in opposition to those descended from the great-grandfather's brother or half-brother but they combine, on other occasions, with these closer collaterals, against others who are genealogically more remote, and so on until hundreds, and thousands, of people are involved. This fusion and fission of genealogical segments is the principle of lineage segmentation.

Lineage segmentation is particularly important as a principle of political structure where central authority is weak or unknown and where, therefore, lineage-members have to provide their own security against others of the same tribe, as well as against outsiders. The political functioning of the lineage system in such tribes can be illustrated from what happens when a member of one lineage kills a member of another in the clan diagrammatically represented below. It is to be remembered that the letters do not represent historic individuals only, but larger or smaller groups of living persons tracing descent from those individuals:

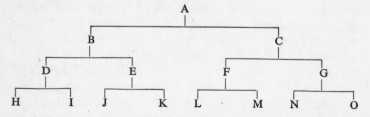

Here the letters represent lineages of different orders, all claiming descent from A, and thence, in the male line, through B, C,

D, E, and so on. If a member of lineage H kills a member of lineage I, then all members of H and all members of I are potentially at enmity with one another. Others are not necessarily involved. But if a member of H or I kills a member of J or K all H and I (now regarding themselves as members of D) may be engaged in hostilities with all J and K (now united as E). So also all B lineage will tend to unite against all C lineage if a man from one kills a man from the other; and finally the whole of A will be united—in theory at least—against outsiders who have injured any one of their members.

Political realities are of course more complex and varied than this paradigm of a lineage system suggests. Among the Arabs, for example, sheikhly families, if with little real power, may introduce some element of personal control into the affairs of lineage segments. Or, as among the Somali, one lineage or group of lineages may have grown numerically and in fighting strength until they outweigh others, of the same descent, with which they were once theoretically more or less equal. The effective balance represented in the paradigm above, and which is often actually maintained among such a people as the Nuer, is upset. As I. M. Lewis has described for the Somali in *A Pastoral Democracy* (1961) other principles then enter into political action in the form of contracts and alliances between different lineages. In some cases, these alliances may even be made between lineages related through women only. Both in logic and in reality, the lineage principle in politics is obviously inconsistent with the centralization of authority since it functions by the distribution of power throughout all the lineage segments. It is not surprising therefore to learn from the same work that the political élite of Somalia, in some ways the most developed of the Somali territories, are reluctant to refer to their clan and lineage affiliations. Even so, we are told, 'despite the self-conscious efforts which are being made in Somalia to weaken the strength of traditional ties and to encourage the growth of wider and less parochial allegiances, contract and clanship . . . continue to rule the lives of the majority'. Modern party politics are still affected by clan affiliations.

Where there is no central authority, or its writ does not run far from the capital, people must right wrongs for themselves without recourse to formally instituted judiciaries or police forces. Councils of elders and chiefs may listen to disputes and express their opinions, stating the traditional rules of conduct of the community, but they have little or no power to enforce those rules.

Therefore where more modern legal procedures have been introduced, the provision of constituted courts has sometimes been welcomed, while their power to implement their decisions has often been resisted. Traditionally in uncentralized societies it was for the plaintiff himself to assert his rights with such support as he could muster from his kin and friends, or for both plaintiff and defendant to accept a reconciliation in the light of a lengthy discussion of the merits of their case. What was of primary public concern was a reconciliation and delimitation of conflict rather than the punishment of an offender. Only when some individual persistently refused to conform to approved standards of behaviour—to be regarded by all as a witch was often a sign of this—did his own kin, even, withdraw their support, and every man's hand might then be raised against him.

Before the effective introduction of modern systems of government, the legal procedures of many peoples did not distinguish between civil and criminal offences. Among the Kipsigis of Kenya, according to J. G. Peristiany's work on these people 'the prosecution ... always proceeds from the individual. There is no such thing as public action in the interests of society.' Each homicide, and indeed any offence or dispute, was considered on its own merits, and according to a more varied range of principles than those applied in modern courts of law. Numerous relations of 'status' between those involved in litigation were more significant in simpler societies than they have come to be in modern states, as Sir Henry Maine observed in the last century. In England to kill a foreigner, or a servant, involves the same penalty as to kill an Englishman or a superior. It was not so in many societies, for the nature of the offence was modified by the relative status of those who were involved in it.

'Status' here does not of course mean exclusively place in a hierarchy of rank or class, but also other kinds of role and position, such as national status, age-status, official status and so forth. What Maine's observation involves (to confine the discussion to the treatment of homicide only) is that where status relations are emphasized, the relative social roles and positions of the killer and the killed are a more significant factor for a judgement on the nature of the offence than under modern types of jurisprudence. In many Arab countries today, killing a wife or sister whose behaviour has been thought to impugn the family honour is treated as a much less serious offence than killing a person not in that relationship to the killer. Again in societies where lineage relations are highly significant, the killing of a member of another lineage genealogically near to one's own, or within the same local community, may be compounded for by the payment of compensation—bloodwealth—to the lineage of the deceased, but the killing of a close kinsman—a brother or half-brother for example—cannot be made up for in this way, for close kinsmen have a common interest in the family wealth. To hand over compensation to the family of a murdered brother would only be offering them what was equally theirs already. Some form of religious expiation by the killer, and perhaps withdrawal to another part of the country, may then be the only solution. But if the killer and the victim are members of distantly related lineages, widely separated communities, or different tribes, peaceful settlement of a case of homicide by the payment of compensation is likely to be impossible. Then vengeance and retaliation are almost inevitable.

For many peoples, then, the ultimate sanction of 'law' is or was self-help, and its object either to reconcile conflicting interests or to achieve reciprocity between the persons or groups involved. The application of the idea of reciprocity is seen in extreme form in the feud. If a member of one lineage kills a member of another, members of the lineage of the dead man have two main courses of action open to them. Either they can accept compensation, in cattle, camels, or other wealth, from the killer's lineage kin, or they can take revenge by killing one of the killer's kinsmen in turn. Men belonging to lineages remote from each other in relationship or territory are more likely to satisfy their honour by taking blood vengeance, taking life for life, sometimes over a period of several generations. This is the feud, which is really a relationship of systematic and long-standing hostility between two lineage groups, involving remote descendants of those concerned in the original killing, who take vengeance when they have the opportunity according to accepted rules which vary from people to people.

Here the right and duty to take life for life is thus vested in the family and the lineage, not in a central authority. What Fustel de Coulanges said of the law of the ancient Greeks and Romans applied to many other peoples of the world until the development of modern government: 'Ancient law was not the work of a legislator; it was on the contrary imposed upon the legislator. It had its birth in the family.' The extreme converse of this wide diffusion of powers was described by de Tocqueville in his famous passage on despotism—an analysis of a state of affairs rarely if ever found in 'primitive' societies:

. . . in a community where the ties of family, of caste, of class and craft fraternities, no longer exist, people are too much disposed to think exclusively of their own interests . . . . Far from trying to counteract such tendencies, despotism encourages them, depriving the governed of any sense of solidarity and interdependence. It immures them, so to speak, each in his private life . . . .

So in studying political life, whether in eighteenth-century France or among the Australian aborigines, we are concerned with the form and diffusion of power and authority, and the social relations in which they are expressed. This examination of internal political *organization* of any particular group is complemented by a study of the external political relations of groups with their neighbours—the political *system* of a whole region.

Systematic relations, of hostility, alliance and so forth, may exist between political units which are not embraced within a single organization. The Nuer among many others have political relations, sometimes expressed in war and raiding and in general hostile, with the neighbouring Dinka. Also Nuer tribes are potentially opposed one to another. Here then is a set of political relations—a political system—involving distinct tribes and peoples; but political *organization* (and in these cases very rudimentary) exists only within each of these tribes.

Each European sovereign state has its political organization—its army, police force and so on—but there is no single organization embracing all these states, though there are systematic political relations between them; and one of the problems involved in the creation and federation of new states is essentially that of converting a political system of relations between once sovereign peoples within its boundaries, into a more comprehensive political organization.

There is a well-documented example of this transformation, the object now of many attempts at conscious planning in the new states of the world, in the way in which the Bedouin tribes of Cyrenaica were united, more by circumstance than design, in the modern state of Libya. The Bedouin of Cyrenaica are divided into several principal tribes, to which there are attached 'client' tribes of different origin. The tribes can place themselves on a single agnatic genealogy which, like all such tribal genealogies, branches out into numerous lineages, which again divide, and subdivide, down to the family.

Traditionally these tribes, though sharing a common culture and an uninstructed form of Islam, were politically opposed to each other. Within each tribe, the component sections, based upon lineages, were similarly opposed. The sheikhs of tribes and sections of tribes seem to have had little authority and no clear order of precedence. Each was the representative of his own group against others: no one had authority to represent or speak for all.

To these people, so divided against themselves, there came a holy man and teacher from outside, Algerian by birth, widely travelled in North Africa, and further educated in Mecca. This man, Sayyid Muhammad bin 'ali al Sanusi—the Grand Sanusi, as he is called—founded a religious order of preachers and teachers devoted to his own particular form of Islamic devotion. In 1843 he founded the first lodge, or settlement, of his order on the central Cyrenaican plateau. From this, 'the White Lodge', his followers proceeded to extend their missionary activities among the Bedouin. Lax in some respects as the religious practice of the Bedouin was, they venerated learned and holy men and saints, whose shrines are places of special devotion in their country, and valued the religious and cultural contribution which members of the Sanusiya Order made to their lives.

The different tribes sought to have lodges of the Order established in their territories and Sanusi settlements were formed, often near wells and springs; the lodges also provided fixed points of reference and social centres for the nomadic Bedouin they served. Other lodges were formed at the oases of the remote interior. The centre of the Order, established at the distant oasis of Jaghbub where the Grand Sanusi retired for contemplation, was by its very position not identified with any one tribe. Hence, a major danger the Order might have faced—that, by being divided between the tribes, it might be itself split by their tribal and sectional rivalries—was surmounted. It retained its unity over and above the diversity of the political groups in which its members were locally settled.

And so for the first time the Bedouin were potentially linked by their common interest in this religious order spread throughout all tribes and sections. More important, that Order itself was organized under a single head and accepted a common discipline. Lands in dispute might be donated to the Order. These were often on the boundaries of tribal territories; and since such land was held sacred, it provided a number of neutral zones where otherwise factional conflict might have been at its greatest, reinforcing the devotion of the Order itself to peacemaking and civilization. Thus by grafting itself on the tribal system of the Bedouin, the Order had roots in their own way of life; but by raising itself above the hostilities inherent in that local system, it gave the Bedouin the possibility of participating in a wider political world than that of their local factions.

The Sanusiya Order developed in Cyrenaica during the period of Turkish administration, and this is of some importance in explaining the form its activities took. The Turks recognized the Order and supported it, leaving to it some of the functions of administration. Because its members were learned men, cosmopolitan in the Arab world, they were able to negotiate in circles of influence quite outside the experience of the Bedouin tribesmen. To use the distinction earlier made, they were able to connect the Bedouin with a wider political *system* of international relations, whilst within Cyrenaica they provided the beginnings of a political *organization* where before there had been but a local political system of opposed tribes and sections.

The culmination of this process came during the periods of Italian invasion, from 1911 to 1917, and from 1923 to 1932. The Turkish administration, though foreign, had been Moslem, and the Turks had therefore roused little serious opposition. The Italians were a different matter, and for the first time the Bedouin were united, and had the need of unity, in opposition to a common enemy. Leadership had already become vested in the Sanusiya Order, and it was the Order which became the focus of opposition and the main object of Italian oppression. At first, they attempted to negotiate with the Head of the Order, thereby recognizing him as, in effect, the head of a government; when this failed, and in the second Italo-Sanusi war, the Order was destroyed within Cyrenaica and its Head and some other representatives fled. From their exile in Egypt, they still provided a symbol of free Cyrenaica, and as such they were recognized by the British during the 1939–45 war. Finally, as is well known, the Head of the Order was recognized as King of Libya. As E. E. Evans-Pritchard concludes in his study of this change from tribal system to state organization through the work of a religious confraternity: 'amid the roar of planes and guns the Bedouin learnt to see themselves more clearly as a single people, the Sanusi of Cyrenaica, in a wider world, and came to be regarded as such by those engaged in the struggle'.

When all historical, cultural, environmental, and personal factors in the rise of the Sanusiya Order have been described we can look at the facts in a simpler, more abstract way, and express them as follows: the common interests and values of a whole people, divided among themselves, were symbolized and represented to the outer world by an organized group (the Sanusiya Order) which shared the local interests of tribes and sections at every point but also transcended their narrow loyalties. And once the political structure of Cyrenaica under the Sanusi has been expressed in this way, it is possible to look for comparable basic structures in other political organizations, even among peoples of totally different culture, environment, and history. One such people are the Shilluk of the Southern Sudan.

The Shilluk are about 120,000 people, living in a densely populated strip of territory along the west bank of the White Nile. Their country is divided, socially, into some hundred settlements, each consisting of a number of hamlets. It is further divided into two main provinces, which unite for the installation of a new king. The Shilluk are also divided by descent into a large number of patrilineal clans, the members of which are dispersed throughout the country in local lineage groups. The largest and most widely distributed clan is the royal clan, tracing descent from the first Shilluk king and culture hero, Nyikang.

Only those sons of the royal clan whose fathers have themselves been installed as kings can claim the kingship in their turn. Consequently there are many members of the royal house who have lost the right to become king; but there are still many legitimate claimants to the royal stools and emblems.

Originally, it seems, there was no single royal capital. A new king reigned from his natal village, which was often his mother's home. Later a royal capital was established at Fashoda, near the centre of the country. There the royal wives live until they become pregnant, when they are sent to provincial villages— often the villages of their own families—to bear their children and bring them up.

Hence there are branches of the royal house, producing claimants to the kingship, in many villages throughout Shillukland, where princes have often replaced the local leaders in political importance. Also, a prince's bid for the kingship, which may traditionally have been either by election or by killing and replacing the reigning king, was supported by the common people of his locality. The princes (unlike the lodges of the Sanusiya Order) were likely to be rivals, but they were united, and united the country, in a common interest in the kingship.

A royal clan here has a position in some ways comparable structurally to that of the Sanusiya Order in Cyrenaica. Its members are acknowledged representatives and leaders in their local political communities, but their relationship with one another also relates the communities to which they belong in a national polity, at the head of which is a religious kingship.

There are many variants of this pattern, or structure, of political relations, in which autonomous and exclusive political segments become united, through a leader who has risen above their oppositions, in a larger political whole. It is a long way from the religious orders of Islam, or the divine kingship of the Shilluk, to religious revivalism in the Pacific islands of Melanesia; but Peter Worsley's account of this in *A Trumpet Shall Sound* (1957) brings out clearly the possibility of discovering similar structural principles under such great diversities of cultural and historical circumstance.

From towards the end of the last century, there have arisen in Melanesia many 'cargo cults' (discussed again in Chap. 6, p. 135) in which a prophet announces that the end of the world is near, and that the people will then get all the European goods they desire from some outside source. The millennium will have come:

The people therefore prepare themselves for the Day by setting up cult-organizations, and by building store-houses, jetties and so on to receive the goods, known as 'cargo' in the local pidgin English. Often, also, they abandon their gardens, kill off their livestock, eat all their food and throw away their money.

Worsley has shown, with explicit reference to such studies as that of the Sanuṣi of Cyrenaica, how the leaders of these movements, religious preachers and prophets, represent a political response by the islanders to foreign wealth and foreign control. The prophet, speaking with a supposedly supernatural authority, is able to provide a focus of allegiance for people who otherwise would be divided and opposed, as members of different little communities each jealous of its neighbours and attached to its local gods and spirits. He is 'reshaping the world', to use an expression from a hymn by the Nuer prophet Ngundeng, as modern state authorities have sometimes tried to fashion the political order anew by more rational planning and action.

The actual power of command vested in those who are nominally rulers, and the ways in which it is exercised, vary very greatly from society to society. Often the trappings and titles of royal office gave Europeans a misleading impression of the effective authority of rulers, who might have little more power to exact obedience than has the queen in a beehive. The Shilluk kings were the symbols of national unity, and their lives so closely bound up with the prosperity of the whole country that when a king died it was said 'there is no land'. But their ability to implement their decisions depended upon calculated collaboration with influential provincial leaders, and they could intervene in the judgement of legal cases only by throwing the weight of their personal support on one side rather than another. They could not command absolutely, from above. This situation is brought to life in a passage from a Somali poem translated by I. M. Lewis and B. W. Andrzejewski:

You two lineages,
Hurling boasts of strength in each other's teeth;
We are more tightly bound as kinsmen than any other group
And yet there is rancour amongst us.
We remember the battle of 'Anla
And the five (we lost); amongst them 'Aadle
And the first-born son of my mother
And 'Ali Fiin, we have not forgotten,
And those killed in a desolate place
Were kinsmen to us,
And Jaama', loved by all
And our leading spokesman,
And Rabjaan, both in revelry
And in defiance of our custom you killed,
And now if you start to devour each other
I will not stand aloof
But adding my strength to one side
I shall join in the attack on the other.
Oh clansmen, stop the war![1]

1. From I. M. Lewis and B. W. Andrzejewski, *Somali Poetry*, 1964.

The British administrative policy of Indirect Rule, intended to preserve indigenous political institutions in the interests of a more economical and humane foreign control, could succeed fully only in states where native rulers had already acquired considerable powers of coercion. Elsewhere chiefs confirmed in office because they appeared to enjoy popular confidence were ground between the upper millstone of a colonial government and the lower of their own people. 'It was the conduct of hereditary chiefs which the official found beyond the pale of understanding,' wrote the Master of Bellhaven in his reminiscences of Aden, *The Kingdom of Melchior* (1949):

They were given rifles to restore order in their territories. They used them in the prosecution of private feuds, they sold them to the highest bidder and on several occasions they gave them away as bribes. They did not appear to understand the word 'rule'. They were in fact shy of ruling. When one talked of strengthening their power they made excuses, changed the subject or looked the other way, as if one had said something indecent.

Nor was it necessarily a high regard for democratic or constitutional legitimacy which made such leaders reluctant to assert and extend their control. Leaders who exceeded their traditional scope risked their followings and their lives in dynastic murders and assassinations. Where, as often, primogeniture is not the invariable custom, there are several claimants at any time to the highest office in chiefly families, and alternative rulers are readily available. Frequent rebellion has been a feature of such politics. Unlike revolution, rebellion does not seek to overthrow the whole system of rule, and may be held, as M. Gluckman and others have said, to confirm popular approval for it, since in substituting one legitimate claimant to chieftaincy for another the 'rebels' indicate their regard for the established office.

A favourite subject of earlier anthropologists, as of political scientists and philosophers, was the Origin of the State; and though it is no longer hoped to reduce the varied forms of this institution to any single original, or establish a universal process of development, it is still profitable to examine the condi-

tions in which central political authority of various kinds has
emerged in essentially egalitarian societies like those so far
described.

Even in the least centralized polities, individuals and families
have achieved prominence as leaders, if only for short periods
and particular ends. Among the Nuer any form of government
by chiefs was unknown, and a balance of force between section
and section, tribe and tribe, prevented any one from dominating the rest. This equality was consistent with other features of
Nuer life—economic insecurity, ethnic and cultural homogeneity, and difficult communications. Even when the first experiments in elective local government were made in 1951, each
representative tended to act as spokesman for the exclusive interest of his own section against all others. The oppositions
which had maintained the egalitarianism of the traditional
system reappeared in committees and courts intended to take
collective responsibility for government.

But in Nuer history, prophets, speaking for God and rising
above their narrow sectional patriotisms, had been able to rally
not only different sections, but different tribes, against their
common enemies; and on a smaller scale small lineages of
priests, who stood somewhat outside the main political oppositions of their communities, were able to arbitrate in local
conflicts if invited to do so, urging peace in the name of a higher Power to which both parties might yield without losing
honour. Neither priests nor prophets *ruled*; but they had moral
and religious authority upon which, in different circumstances,
a wider control might have been based. So also, it will be remembered, the Sanusiya Order in quite a different historical
and cultural setting spread its influence, and the priest (as
Frazer had observed for many other societies) became king.

Where some power of coercion is vested in chieftainship, it
may still be represented by the people themselves as a secondary
rather than primary attribute of rule. The Anuak of the Sudan
and Ethiopia have a royal house which in recent times has acquired fire-arms, and with them in some cases a limited power of
command. According to legend there was at one time no royal
house, and all the Anuak lived under largely ceremonial chief-

tains in separate autonomous village communities, as they do today where the princes have not extended their sway.

The myth of origin of the royal house tells how two boys had seized the same fish in the river, one by the head and the other by the tail. Neither would give way, and the fish escaped. A spirit appeared on a log and told the boys that in future when two caught the same fish, the one who held the tail should relinquish it. When they followed this ruling, they kept their catch. The boys told their chief, who sent his men to fetch the spirit home to the village, where he married the chief's daughter and begat the first Anuak king. The present ruler, Agada, emphasized to me the essential point of this story: that here was the first occasion upon which Anuak had followed a ruling even for their own good, and in doing so they had acknowledged the superior authority and wisdom of the princes.

There are essentially spiritual rulers who, though they may have assumed some secular and military dominance at times, have few and uncertain secular prerogatives. In other kingdoms like those of the Sudanic Azande on the other hand, purely secular kings with real powers of life and death had risen before the foreign invasions, and an empire extended by cultural colonization and military conquest had incorporated many originally distinct groups of peoples under Zande hegemony. But even there the myth of origin of the princely clan tells of a stranger who, overhearing disputes and quarrels among the people around him, gives clear and wise judgements upon them. He is adopted into the local community where he continues to judge cases and dispense hospitality and founds the kingship. Though the Zande, unlike the Anuak, had an aristocracy capable of governing, their government also was seen as originating in a popular consent to princely adjudication.

Each Anuak village exhibits some elements of state-like organization: differentiation of rank and, to some extent, of wealth and occupation, greater than is found among a people like the Nuer; courts of chiefs and princes, not courts of law it is true, but centres for discussion and entertainment, with a formal code of behaviour; and the bands of retainers supporting their prince in a personal allegiance, however easily that allegiance may be revoked if he fails to reward them, are features of a rudimentary state-like polity. To these the Zande kings add real judicial functions and powers, a more elaborate military organization at the king's command, and a system of communications from the provinces to the capital enabling many districts to be incorporated in a single national political organization.

But the Anuak, and even the Azande, remain in some respects democratic and egalitarian as compared with the Interlacustrine Bantu kingdoms of Uganda. Neither among the Anuak nor the Azande were the princes the personal owners, except in a symbolic sense, of their lands, and there was no peasantry subject to overlords by dependence upon them for the tenure of land. There were differences of rank, but not of class; the princes were leaders rather than masters, even among the Azande, and the system upon which authority was delegated was far less formal and elaborate than in the Bantu kingdoms.

These kingdoms—Buganda, Bunyoro, Ankole, Toro, and also Rwanda and Burundi—in their different ways have developed systems of rule, and of social stratification, which are held to derive from conquering pastoral aristocracies established as the 'feudal' overlords of indigenous agricultural populations. If the myth of the founding of the royal house of Bunyoro, for example, be compared with those of Anuak and Azande already reported, something of this difference in outlook is revealed.

The Nyoro myth as reproduced in John Beattie's neat monograph *Bunyoro, An African Kingdom* (1960) tells that in the first human family there were three sons who initially had no names of their own. God was asked to give them names to distinguish them. He did so by offering them a choice from a selection of objects, and by ordering them to sit all night holding bowls of milk without spilling them. The eldest son chose a bundle of food, a ring for carrying burdens on the head, and an axe and a knife. He also spilt all his milk during the night. The second son chose a leather thong. During the night, he gave a little milk to his younger brother to replace a little that the youngest had spilt. The youngest chose an ox's head, and though he spilt some of his milk, this was made up by his brother and his pot alone therefore was full in the morning.

The eldest son's choice is that of the peasant and servant, and his spilling of milk shows him unfit to tend cattle. He and his descendants must therefore be servants and peasants. The second son's choice establishes him and his descendants with the dignity of cattle-herders. The youngest son's choice, the ox's head, and his full pot of milk, identify him as the head of all men, and he and his descendants are therefore kings.

Here in myth is a charter (in Malinowski's language) for the differentiation of the people of Bunyoro into hereditary classes of superiors and inferiors. There is a 'premise of inequality' which according to J. J. Maquet is the outstanding feature of these Interlacustrine polities.

The systems of political relations and forms of rule touched on in this chapter are but a few of those which emerge in the comparative anthropological study of politics, but they serve to suggest the differences—some bold and striking, some more subtle and scientifically interesting—existing within the field. The non-literate societies of the world, even those of Africa alone, exhibit different experience of practical politics, from which different political philosophies and political ideals might have been deduced had professional intellectuals been there to reflect on them. These 'primitive' polities have however one characteristic in common as against the polities of modern mass civilization: the intensely personal conduct of political affairs. Competition for favour, jealousies and rivalries, a quickness of all members of society to assert their rights and promote their interests against the world, provide or provided ready conditions for division and secession. Rulers neglected their standing with common people at immediate risk to their position. From the king downwards, those in authority were expected to be readily accessible to their people, to whom also they were personally bound in many ways—by kinship and inter-marriage, by neighbourliness, and by the reciprocal gifts and services which are the subjects of the chapter which follows.

4

Economics and Social Relations

A few words, touching presents to African princes, the sole object
of whose foreign friendships is to obtain them, and with whom
those who pay highest are, and ever will be, the most powerful. . . .

Sir Richard Burton, *A Mission to Dahomey*

POLITICAL AND ECONOMIC AFFAIRS were closely connected in non-industrial societies as in our own, as was recognized
more clearly by Sir Richard Burton in his dealings with the
King of Dahomey than by his government at home: 'It is commonly thought in England that anything is good enough for a
barbarian: and I have seen presents sent out which a West
African Chief would hardly think of giving to his slave.' Indeed, the immediacy of the connexion between economic and
other human relations is more apparent in simple societies, without the complex commercial organization and elaborate financial and fiscal systems which depersonalize economic transactions in the industrial world.

The social anthropologists then must take into account aspects of social behaviour which do not directly concern modern
professional economists—the exchange of gifts, the co-operation of kin and neighbours, the religious and magical rites
which often encourage and co-ordinate labour, and the feasting
and display which are important ends and motives of production.

To understand these is particularly urgent where, as over
much of the world at the present day, traditional ways of gain-

ing a living, and traditional views of the nature and uses of wealth, are being replaced by wage-earning in an industrial world. In *The Great Village* (1957), C. S. Belshaw has written of the condition of the Hanuabadans of New Guinea, once horticulturalists but now existing in slums around Port Moresby and labouring for cash. This way of making a living thwarts some of the more important ambitions of the traditional Hanuabadan life:

the Hanuabadan does not gain very much prestige by succeeding in the wage-earning world. The criteria of success in the labouring world are not those of village life. Here it is the making of a proper marriage and the fulfilment of family and ceremonial obligations that counts. . . .

And the conclusion drawn by Raymond Firth from Belshaw's study would apply to many agricultural and pastoral peoples moving from subsistence economies to a money economy, for whom the economic basis of life is changing more rapidly than traditional moral values:

. . . production in Hanuabada . . . is geared as much to self-respect and prestige within the community as to the possibility of increased personal consumption. Unless this is understood by those who are trying to raise the Melanesian economic level, their efforts are bound to meet with much frustration.

Working with simple tools and often in hard environments, many peoples have never been able to accumulate and store any regular surplus. Hunting and collecting groups—living from month to month and even from day to day on the products of their labour—are extreme examples of the hand-to-mouth existence characteristic of subsistence economies in their simplest form. In an article on the utilization of food resources by an Australian aboriginal tribe Peter Worsley has shown in detail how incessantly they search for food, and how quickly even a large animal is consumed by friends and relatives who come from far to share the good fortune of the hunters:

Hunting in consequence is an ingrained habit. No opportunity is ever missed of procuring food: walks along the sea coast are constantly interrupted for spear-throws at fish, irrespective of the state of the larder or one's stomach. Once a party carrying a corpse to the cemetery with due reverence, detailed off one of its members to spear some fish observed in the water.

Worsley has also drawn attention to the elementary principles of conserving natural resources common among such peoples, as when a small piece of the tuber of the wild yam is left in the ground to provide for the next year.

There are also much richer subsistence economies in which a regular surplus is produced. They are found where some degree of technological advance, combined with favourable environmental conditions, some exportable materials, and a simple marketing system, have permitted such a development. Though both the poorer and the richer economies founded upon producing primarily for local consumption are equally subsistence economies in contrast to money or market economies, they differ markedly between themselves. In Ancient Egypt and the lands of the Fertile Crescent, in parts of India and South-East Asia, in the trading kingdoms of West Africa and elsewhere, a peasant economy at subsistence level has formed the basis of more elaborate economic systems. The accumulation of surpluses and their unequal distribution has been associated with more complex political development, greater social stratification, and a richer proliferation of the arts and artefacts than are associated with simple subsistence.

In non-industrial societies—even where trade plays some part—the redistribution of wealth is primarily a simple, direct transaction between the poorer and the richer. One man's surplus is used to relieve the wants of his kin, his friends, his neighbours, as happens certainly among the poorer sections of the population in the modern industrial world. This sharing of the necessities of life is an insurance against local failures of the food supply and individual misfortunes. Where life is precarious from year to year, and generosity is high among the virtues, it is in the interest of all to give when they can, so that they may receive when they must.

The practical necessity in some societies to relieve the wants of others, may further be recognized as a binding religious duty. So the *zakat*, or legal alms, which are demanded of Moslems, rank in religious importance with prayer and fasting; what is due in alms-giving is doctrinally defined. Whatever the practice, the *rule* is that one-fifth of the value of buried treasure, for example, or of the value of metals taken from mines, must be given to the needy. Religious prescription has here an economic function.

The preparedness to share, and the complications of joint-ownership found in simpler societies, were at one time interpreted as 'primitive communism'. The expression obscures the real situation. As Malinowski wrote of the system of land-holding found among the Trobriand Islanders:

Almost to spite the anthropological theorists, the Trobriander insists upon having his own plot associated with his personal name. This old opposition between individual and communal ownership is a vicious and unintelligent short-cut because . . . the real problem before us was not the either-or of individualism and communism, but the relation of collective and personal claims.

Even the little hunting and collecting bands of the Negritos of Malaya regard certain wild trees as the property of particular individuals, who own their fruits, and come to regard the place where their trees are as their own tiny estates.

Social anthropologists like others studying the notion of property have found it necessary to break down the notion of 'ownership' and discuss it as a matter of different kinds of rights. The Interlacustrine Bantu in particular have suggested many comparisons with feudalism in Europe. Thus among the Banyoro already mentioned there were three broad categories of rights in land. First, the whole land and everything in it 'belonged' to the ruler, the Mukama, by right ultimately of conquest. Then those to whom the Mukama made grants of estates had the rights in them which he had granted. These landowners, or rather land-holders, were territorial chiefs and sub-chiefs. Then finally there were rights in land vested in the clan heads, who without 'ownership' were entitled to cultivate the earth and have the usufruct. Accounts of the extremely complicated rights in water supplies in Ceylon, Spain, amongst the Arabs and others who depend on irrigation also show that it is impossible to understand these rights and the sets of social relations they involve in terms of any kind of outright overall personal ownership of supplies.

Where there has been economic security and rulers have been able to accumulate surplus wealth and augment their status by it, that wealth has still traditionally been used in large part for their people. The British Columbian Indians, with their rich and certain harvests of fish, produced leaders whose standing and following depended upon vast expenditure in feasting and entertaining, and who might on occasion totally impoverish themselves to achieve social prestige. Malinowski reported that in the Trobriand Islands over 20,000 baskets of yams were presented to one chief by his people in a single year. These yams clearly could not all be eaten by his family, nor could they be stored for long or sold in quantity, so in fact there was little alternative but to distribute them with lavish generosity. Many African rulers knew well that they could not for long retain the allegiance of their people if they were unprepared or unable to redistribute among them much of the wealth derived from chiefly office. The Bemba of central Africa speak for many other peoples when, as Audrey Richards reports, they say: 'We will shake the tree until it gives up its fruit,' meaning that people will worry the chief until he gives them what they want: 'If a chief attempted to dry meat and keep if for subsequent division, his followers would sit and stare at him and talk about it until he was forced to give them some.'

With changes from subsistence to money economy, greater emphasis is of course placed on individual acquisitiveness and self-sufficiency. Chiefs have been known to sell surpluses which at one time they would have shared out among their people and on the side of the people themselves expectation of cash payment for labour replaces service in return for feasting and gifts. Yet the moral values of a subsistence economy, and belief in the mutual assistance and co-operation which go with such an economy, linger on among many wage-earners, as among the Hanuabadans.

In the very nature of their material, social anthropologists have been forced to draw attention to the positive social function of customs which, if looked at from a purely economic point of view, appear irrational and sometimes ruinously wasteful. This approach does not, as is sometimes supposed, spring from any anthropological desire to conserve exotic customs, but from experience of the interdependence of social institutions. As those who have official responsibility for directing social change have sometimes found out to their cost, institutions of which they approve are often inseparably connected with customs which they would prefer to abolish, and an ill-considered measure which appears to be for the good may produce effects quite other than those intended.

One of the most familiar anthropological examples of the non-economical use of wealth was to be found among the Indians of the coasts of British Columbia in an institution called *potlatch*. These Indians, immensely rich by the standards of even the wealthiest subsistence economies, had a most elaborate system of rank and status. This was largely maintained by display and competition in gargantuan feasting and entertainments, where from time to time persons of distinction would *potlatch*— that is, give away or even destroy vast quantities of their possessions. Of these the most highly regarded were plaques or sheets of copper, of no intrinsic utilitarian value, but counted worth great numbers of blankets and other useful goods. Though blankets, cloth, fish oil, and other commodities dispensed on a wildly extravagant scale in *potlatch* were, unlike the 'coppers', potentially useful, they were accumulated by the rich in such quantities that their owners had little use for them outside the *potlatch* situation.

The purpose of this entertainment and distribution of gifts was to assert relative social standing and compete for higher and higher prestige. The recipients at a *potlatch* 'party' were required by custom to accept the gifts; and in order not to lose face they 'fought' to outdo their previous host when, after perhaps a year, their turn to *potlatch* came round. A good indication of the scale of this obligatory gift-exchange is to be found in Helen Codere's monograph *Fighting with Property* (1950), where *potlatches* are recorded in which thousands and tens of thousands of blankets, as well as many other commodities, have been given away. The Indians' enthusiasm for the non-utilitarian

copper plaques is conveyed by a traditional account of a very
large copper, which had come to represent, in terms of exchange, more or less limitless riches:

. . . there was nothing that was not paid for it. It made the house
empty. Twenty canoes was its price; and twenty slaves was its price;
and also ten coppers tied to the end was its price, and twenty lynx
skins, and twenty marmot skins, and twenty sewed blankets was its
price; and twenty mink blankets was its price; and one hundred
boards was its price; and forty wide planks was its price; and twenty
boxes of dried berries added to it and twenty boxes of clover. . . .

and the list continues, giving a very direct impression of the
nature of the wealth of that Indian culture.

The Administration made strong efforts to forbid and dis-
courage *potlatch* on economic and other grounds, and in some
cases indeed it reached such a pitch of wastefulness, in manic
competitions by the actual destruction of property—breaking
coppers or throwing them into the sea, and burning blankets
and oil—that it is easy to see the administrative point of view.
Yet the Indians clung to their custom, as when one Indian chief
said to Boas:

We will dance when our laws command us to dance, we will feast
when our hearts desire to feast. Do we ask the white man, 'Do as the
Indian does'? No, we do not. Why then do you ask us 'Do as the
white man does'? It is a strict law that bids us dance. It is a strict law
that bids us distribute our property among our friends and neighbours. It is a good law. Let the white man observe his law, we shall
observe ours. And now, if you are come to forbid us to dance, be-
gone, if not, you will be welcome to us.

Helen Codere has shown that the *potlatch*, from the European
point of view a form of madness, was the basis of a complex
social organization which could not be maintained without it.
The heavy expenditure it made necessary could not have been
undertaken without an intricate system of loans, credit, and
interest. Indebtedness, as anthropologists have often pointed
out, is a form of relationship with many integrating social functions. To abolish *potlatch* then was nor merely to abolish an

isolated wasteful custom, but to destroy the system of ranking in the society, the relations between tribes and their chiefs, even the relations between friends and kinsmen. The pattern of social interdependence which the Indians had created and valued would have been radically altered. Further, as some of the people themselves recognized, the destructive *potlatch* was a substitute for warfare, proscribed by the Administration, and certainly even less acceptable to those responsible for government than the *potlatch* itself. An Indian said: 'When I was young I have seen streams of blood shed in war. But since that time the white man came and stopped up that stream of blood with wealth. Now we are fighting with our wealth.' He might well have understood some of the international loans and gifts made by the Great Powers in our own time as they bid for influence.

Extravagance and display in the use of wealth in modern industrial society, and competition for power and prestige there in some ways comparable to that found among the Indians, engaged the interest of the nineteenth-century American sociologist and economist Thorstein Veblen. Veblen introduced the expression 'conspicuous consumption' for the competitive use of wealth to establish and validate social status. His *The Theory of a Leisure Class* (1899) is a wider-ranging survey and analysis of the relation between wealth, labour, social prestige, and power, based upon his observation that activities economically and practically unproductive—fox-hunting might be an example— often carried high social prestige, while productive labour was often a mark of lower social status. So in his own American society useless objects (comparable to the coppers of the North-West Coast Indians) were frequently accorded higher value, and conferred greater prestige on their owners, than merely utilitarian articles. With much attention to details of social behaviour in the America and Europe of his time, Veblen argued that the highest social prestige was accorded to those who did not need to work in order to live. In the economic competition for power (which he attributed to a surviving predatory instinct) those were most likely to succeed who had the marks of inherited wealth and leisure.

Even in attitudes towards pets, Veblen found some confirmation for his idea that expensive uselessness was a criterion of value:

The dog, then, commends himself to our favour by affording play to our propensity for mastery, and as he is also an item of expense, and commonly serves no industrial purpose, he holds a well assured place in men's regard as a thing of good repute. The dog is at the same time associated with the chase—a meritorious employment and an expression of the honourable predatory impulse.

As for fancy-breeds in animals generally, their value was correlated with their peculiarity, and the trouble which had to be taken to produce it:

The commercial value of canine monstrosities, such as the prevailing styles of pet dogs both for men's and women's use, rests upon their high cost of production, and their value to their owners lies chiefly in their utility as items of conspicuous consumption. Indirectly, through reflection on their honorific expensiveness, a social worth is imputed to them. . . .

In preferred types of female beauty, and in female fashion in which he took a great interest, Veblen also found confirmation of his theories. 'Robust, large-limbed women' were preferred for useful tasks, and therefore, as servants; but higher in prestige was the 'lady', symbol of wealth and leisure, 'infirmly delicate, translucent, and hazardously slender' whose constricting costume, like the deformed feet of high-born Chinese, indicated her expensive uselessness. But in his own time, Veblen observed, the delicate woman was losing ground in favour of 'the archaic type that does not disown her hands and feet, nor, indeed, the other gross material facts of her person', because 'under the higher efficiency of modern industry, leisure in women is possible so far down the social scale of reputability that it no longer serves as a definitive mark of the highest pecuniary grade'.

Veblen's analysis of course rests on deeper and more serious foundations than these. In his opposition to simply pecuniary standards of value, he would have had much in common with members of many so-called primitive societies. But in his implied, and sometimes open, criticism of 'conspicuous consumption', and of the value and prestige attached to the economically

and practically useless, he would have been opposed to characteristics of human behaviour which are much more widespread
even in comparatively simple societies than he seems to have
recognized. The luxurious entertainments of his modern rich,
their attachment to possessions of purely ceremonial and aesthetic value, their competition to transform wealth into power,
all bear a resemblance to the Indian *potlatch* and Melanesian yam
display.

They relate in part also to another 'economic' institution that
has attracted a great deal of anthropological attention, again
from Melanesia—the *kula* trading and exchange ring of the Tro-
briands and other Melanesian Islands.

Twice a year or so, when time could be spared from horticulture, each island would launch a canoe-party to visit others
across the ocean. Elaborate practical and magical preparations
were made for these often arduous journeys, on which the
voyagers carried gifts for their friends abroad, and local
specialities for barter—pots, for example, were made in some
islands and not in others.

But these were not simple trading expeditions, for the main
object of the islanders was to acquire two kinds of objects
which had no direct practical use—special kinds of armlet made
of white shell, and of necklace made of red shell. These were
the real treasures, the jewels as it were, of the islands.

Arriving at their destination, the travellers were entertained
by their hosts, handed over their gifts, and bartered their goods.
But the men most esteemed in the party would also and more
importantly seek from regular partners (who were made for
life) the white shell armlets or the red shell necklaces. These
were carried back, from island to island, the armlets always
travelling roughly in one direction and the necklaces in
another in a constant cycle of exchange.

In receiving or giving these objects, no haggling was allowed.
With many formalities, they were received and bestowed to
mark the regard the partners to exchange had one for the
other. And since some time elapsed between the gift and the
counter-gift, each giver displayed the confidence—the credit,
in fact—which his partner could command. And the partners

performed many arcane magical rites to ensure the affection, regard, and generosity of those with whom they made these exchanges, for their own prestige and self-esteem depended upon the beauty and fame of the particular examples of these two kinds of valuable—not all being regarded as equally precious—which their partners entrusted to them.

In a group of islands then, partners to this exchange relationship are circulating shell armlets from island to island in one direction, and circulating the shell necklaces in another, though the whole pattern of this exchange may not be apparent to any individual islander. This circulation of items which have no other trading value—they can be exchanged only for each other—is however *accompanied* by trade and barter, and by regular social relations between islanders, who without the *kula* ring, would have no need or incentive to leave their own islands.

Here again then, objects of no utilitarian value are a form, even the very type, of wealth, and the giving and receiving of them has many practical social consequences. In *Argonauts of the Western Pacific* (1922) Malinowski first perceived that this particular Melanesian institution, at first sight so strange, required a reassessment of the materialistic conceptions of some of his predecessors in the study of primitive economics, a revaluation of the notion of economic man who 'always knows where his material interests lie, and makes for them in a straight line'. Malinowski's research into what might have been represented simply as a quaint custom of remote peoples did indeed do something, as he hoped, 'to dispel such crude rationalistic conceptions of primitive mankind, and to induce both the speculator and the observer to deepen the analysis of economic facts'. As he says,

the Kula shows us that the whole conception of primitive value; the very incorrect habit of calling all objects of value 'money' or 'currency'; the current ideas of primitive trade and primitive ownership—all these have to be revised in the light of our institution.

Modern attitudes towards 'money', and ideas about its nature, have indeed caused a good deal of misunderstanding of the economic transactions of traditional societies. In the many varied types of exchange recorded in ethnographic writings, we rarely if ever find any one kind of unit of value that serves, like our money, as a common denominator of value for all others. The Maori set a great value on their greenstone (in this case also of practical use), which since it was portable and imperishable, was also used in exchange. Hence Europeans and modernized Maori considered it to be Maori 'money'; but Raymond Firth has said that 'it was at no time a common measure of values, nor did it even act as a medium of exchange to facilitate trans- actions in other articles'. Any resemblance between the func- tion of greenstone in exchange, and the function of money, was hence superficial and marginal.

There are also many examples of objects with a restricted sphere of exchange—that is, objects which can be exchanged with some other objects but not with others. Shells may be ex- changed for shells, but not for food and so on. In our own society, it is easier to conceive of exchanging, say, a Chinese vase for some other work of art, than to think of exchanging it directly for clothing or cooking utensils. In the latter exchange, assessment of the relative exact monetary value of the units of exchange would enter more importantly than in the former.

The very idea of buying and selling with fixed prices and standards of value was strange to many peoples. E. E. Evans- Pritchard records that the Nuer, when 'buying' from Arab merchants, regard the purchase as an exchange of gifts: '... what is involved in an exchange of this kind is a relation between per- sons rather than between things. It is the merchant who is "bought" rather than the goods, just as it is God or a spirit who is bounden by sacrifice.' And, among the Nuer, the same word is used for the transaction of 'purchase'—both 'buying' *and* 'selling'—and for offerings to God.

With such facts in mind, we can easily see that much eco- nomic theory derived from economic operations in modern societies would not be properly applicable in others. George Dalton, writing in *The American Anthropologist* (Vol. 63, No.1), has suggested that 'in the Western meaning of the word, there is no "economy" in primitive society, only socio-economic in- stitutions'. There is no 'market' in the economist's sense of the word, and for that reason there is no 'money': 'It is only when land and labor, as well as fabricated goods, are organized as available commodities to be bought and sold through the market mechanism that a money economy exists.' But as Dalton also recognizes, economists and anthropologists might meet in the study of changes now increasingly being brought about in societies which until recently had no developed market in this sense:

Western economic theory has proved a powerful tool for making industrialized market systems grow. But primitive economies are neither industrialized nor market systems. One must start from ethno-economic analysis—with Malinowski, not Ricardo—in order to choose those transformation paths to industrialization which entail only the unavoidable social costs.

The literature on such changes in many parts of the world shows how high the costs—some of them surely avoidable— may be.

It might still be held that the whole complex of exchange involved in such institutions as the *kula* and *potlatch* is so different from any of the concerns of modern technical economists that it scarcely touches upon matters of professional concern to them. Veblen did not think so; and more recently, writing of modern social problems in his *Economic Theory and Underdeveloped Regions*, Gunnar Myrdal has in effect stated the position reached by students of the simpler societies, when they are forced to consider how far, for them, economic processes can reasonably be isolated from others:

. . . it is useless to look for any one predominant factor, a 'basic factor' such as the 'economic factor'. When studying the Negro problem [in the U.S.A.] or any other problem under this hypothesis it becomes, indeed, difficult to perceive what precisely should be meant by the 'economic factor' as distinct from the others, and still less understandable how it can be 'basic', as everything is cause to everything else in an interlocking circular manner.

A direct connexion between labour, food, wealth, and pleasure and marriage—between 'economic' and other factors—is charmingly expressed in a Yoruba poem for example:

New yam causes the wife of yesterday to lose her manners,
New yam causes the head of the household to reject food.
It makes a rich person speak out. [break wind]
Yam will pay its own debt.
[New yam says] 'Lay me on a fine bed
And I will lay you on a fine lady'.

And the inseparability of economic from such other social factors was emphasized in a short but very significant study of exchanges, gifts, and notions of value by Marcel Mauss—his *Essai sur le Don* (1925) (translated as *The Gift*, by I. G. Cunnison, 1954). Mauss had observed in the course of very wide reading how many gifts, or more widely 'prestations' as he called them, were in fact obligatory and reciprocal. This was clearly so among the Melanesians and the British Columbian Indians; and a moment's reflection reminds us that in modern commercialized society, there still remains an element of shame and embarrassment, even loss of face and influence, in failing to make any return for birthday or Christmas gifts, or for hospitality.

Prestige, generosity, affection, and other social and moral elements are all involved in the situation of giving, exchanging, and even paying. There are occasions when to pay or return everything one owes is a sign of severing all relationships, a sign of hostility. The prestige involved in paying is shown in extreme form in a case of murder recorded a few years ago in Iraq, where two friends took a taxi, which neither would allow the other to pay for. One shot the other. They were, it is true, tipsy.[1]

Such uses of and attitudes towards wealth could not, as Mauss perceived, be at all adequately understood in terms of a theoretical 'economic man', giving as little and receiving as much as possible, and assumed in some older and purely economic theory. Malinowski, as we have seen, had come to the same conclusion, but Mauss sets his findings in a wider sociological and psychological context, and presses much further towards a general theoretical consideration of the very notion of value

[1] From 'Homicide in Iraq', unpublished thesis by Dr Noori Kadhim.

itself. And here he comes to the conclusion, strange at first sight if we are thinking of modern economic transactions, that economic value has a religious origin. This had been the suggestion of Durkheim also when, towards the end of *The Elementary Forms of the Religious Life*, he stated in a footnote:

Only one form of social activity has not yet been expressly attached to religion: that is, economic activity . . . economic value is a sort of power or efficacy, and we know the religious origins of the idea of power. Also, richness can confer *mana*, sacredness; therefore it has it. Hence it is to be seen that the idea of economic value and that of religious value ought not to be unconnected. But the question of the nature of these connections has not yet been studied.

Mauss's work did something to expand the original, self-confessedly obscure perception of Durkheim, but since that time its possible sociological significance, and relevance to more orthodox approaches to the study of economic value, have received less attention than they may deserve. They were to have been a major field of investigation for a very gifted Czech sociologist and social anthropologist, Franz Steiner, whose early death in 1952 prevented him from completing much original work. Before his death however he had sketched out some of his ideas in a brief article, *Notes on Comparative Economics*, later published in *The British Journal of Sociology* (1954). This study deserves more consideration than its modest title might attract.

Like Mauss (and following the principles of the writers of the *Année Sociologique*) Franz Steiner proceeds from concrete example, referring first to a reported conversation between a rich herdsman of the Yurak-Samoyede and a stranger:

Stranger: Sell me a reindeer!
Yurak: There is none for sale.
Stranger: Why don't you take money? You may buy brandy with it.
Yurak: I have got brandy enough.
Stranger: You may buy something for your womenfolk; or you may get furs of arctic fox to use as bridewealth and get yourself another wife.
Yurak: I have got two sledges full of fox already.

Stranger: You own 3,000 reindeer. What are you keeping them for?
Yurak: The reindeer wander about and I look at them. Money I have
  to hide, I cannot see it.

These attitudes towards wealth, particularly in stock, are widespread. What are their implications for the understanding of
non-monetary economies?

Steiner was particularly interested in the variety of forms of
exchange recorded in the ethnographic literature, and had been
specially struck by the conversion of units of empirical or
practical value into units of ritual or ceremonial value, a process
which he called 'translation'. Thus in the *potlatch*, goods given
away are translated into social status; those who receive them
dispose of their utilitarian value, those who give them renounce
that utilitarian value in favour of enhanced social status. When
goods are completely destroyed, their empirical values are elimi-
nated and absolutely converted into social, ceremonial, or ritual
value. In such cases (and the Yurak-Samoyede's 'wastefulness'
in not using his great herds of reindeer has a comparable
quality) Steiner observed that the ritual or ceremonial values
into which wealth of various kinds could be translated, transcended the utilitarian or empirical values of the society, and
that these transcending values were created by a conspicuous
rejection of utilitarian values. So among the Yap Islanders (to
use one of his examples) large accumulations of goods were
periodically exchanged for great circular plates of stone with
religious importance, which were buried under the huts of their
owners and served simply to increase the respect shown to
them. One may see, perhaps, some parallel with the stockpiling
of armaments. Again, among the Trobriand Islanders, vast
quantities of yams, according to Malinowski, were stored for
display and deliberately not used. (Here it should be said that it
has since been reported that it is inevitable in the technique of
yam cultivation, that great surpluses should accumulate in some
years. Nevertheless Malinowski shows that the Trobrianders
deliberately practice self-denial in yam-consumption, performing magical rites to reduce their appetite for yams: 'They will
boast that when this magic is performed well, half of the yams

will rot away in the store-houses and be thrown on . . . the rubbish heap.')

This transcending of purely utilitarian value, according to Steiner, does not stop in the simpler societies:

After all, the conquest of Western Civilisation by a total money economy meant the bestowing of transcending values on money. The holding of money, the position in which a person's money is 'working' for him and does not lie 'idle', are aims the evaluation of which transcends the evaluation of the goods which can be purchased with this money and used. The rise of capitalist economy came in the guise of a gospel of saving, and ascetic rejection of the use of goods. No reader of the works of Max Weber and Tawney can doubt the fact that this ascetic rejection was postulated in a religious terminology.

Here, then, in the connexion between the sacrificing of material property, or self-denial in the use of it, and ritual or ceremonial status, Steiner sought the link between notions of economic and of religious value, which Durkheim and Mauss had earlier considered to be a major problem for sociological investigation. There remains a large field for the economic anthropologist to explore. When the simpler societies enter the modern economic world, their own forms of wealth are often devalued. They become poor in relation to much of the new world they have entered. How far is this poverty connected with a disintegration of the older form of society? Anthropological evidence would suggest that it is an important factor, and Steiner himself suggested that:

After the first European war an inflation caused the loss of property of the German middle classes. This was followed in Protestant Germany by a complete disintegration not merely of what Weber called *Wirtschaftsethik* (itself a Protestant departmentalization) but by the disintegration of the whole ideals and codes of the middle classes. No short-lived hardship, however severe, can account for loss of confidence on such a scale.

Similarly, as much anthropological evidence shows (one example is the plight of the Hanuabadans discussed on p. 75, but one could also consider, say, the social effects of African labour migration), the impact of a Western economy on simpler societies has been accompanied by a kind of inflation in their own economy, and by the beginning of a more widespread change in traditional codes and values. And among the most striking and sometimes painful effects of this change are those in domestic life, in the central institutions of any society, marriage and the family.

5

Kinship and Affinity

It is ridiculous that a man should be bound to people through kinship. To your mother and father, yes, you have obligations, for they brought you into the world, but what is a brother, sister or cousin? I recognize ties with no one save the friends of my own choice.   A modern young Spanish gentleman

(from J. A. Pitt-Rivers, *The People of the Sierra*)

THE WEAKNESS AND NARROW RANGE of our family ties and obligations are features of modern suburban life which would have seemed profoundly foreign, and shocking, to the peoples of the ancient world, as they still do to many in Asia, Africa, and Arabia today. The *Antigone* of Sophocles offers a dramatic representation of some of the older attitudes towards kinship, radically opposed to those expressed (for they may not be really held) by modern individualists like the young Spaniard quoted above. Antigone and her sister Ismene are at the court of King Creon, to whose son Antigone is betrothed. Their only two brothers have killed one another in battle, the one fighting for Creon, the other against him. Creon has ordered that the one shall be honoured, while the other shall be left 'unburied, unwept, a feast of flesh for keen-eyed carrion birds'. But Antigone expresses the ultimate duty for her sister and herself, as the only surviving close kin, to give the dishonoured brother's body burial, and asks Ismene to help her:

Antigone: Will you help me? Will you do something with me? Will you?

Ismene: Help you do what, Antigone? What do you mean?
Antigone: Would you help me lift the body ... you and me?
Ismene: You cannot mean ... to bury him? Against the order?
Antigone: Is he not my brother and yours, whether you like it
      Or not? I shall never desert him, never.

Ismene dares not disobey the order of the king. She hovers
between conflicting demands of family and state in a way perhaps more natural to modern eyes than Antigone's single-
minded self-committal to the overriding claims of kin. Antigone buries her brother by herself, and is put to death for doing
so—'convicted of reverence', as she has earlier said.

In the eyes of Sophocles and his audience, Antigone was
right in placing a task imposed upon her by kinship and by religious precept above the rule of the state. Creon is punished as a
tyrant for exacting an obedience, to him as ruler, which denies
the priority of the most solemn duties of kindred. These were
regarded as absolutely binding, as they would ideally be today
by many peoples outside the metropolitan Western world. For
many still 'kinship ... is one of the irreducible principles upon
which their organized social life depends', as Professor Fortes
observed in writing of the Tallensi of northern Ghana. To the
anthropologist also kinship is something more than one aspect
of social life which can be conveniently isolated for separate
consideration. An understanding of it forms a necessary ground-
work for the study of all other social activities.

While mating is a fact of the biological order, marriage is
uniquely a creation of human society. Similarly, the family, and
more widely kinship, are social, not biological conceptions. In
modern urban conditions in Britain, the basic domestic family
unit of a father, a mother, and their children does often correspond to a biological unit of male, female, and their offspring.
Even then, however, not every group properly called a family
is thus biologically related—there are adoptions and foster
parents, for example—nor does every fertile union of man and
woman produce a co-residential family in the social sense. And
among many peoples of the world they do so much less. An
extreme example is found among the Nayars of Malabar, whose
'marriage' is a form of union known as polyandry—a form

which is relatively rare—in which several men are simultaneously the 'husbands' of a single wife, whose company they
share between them according to conventional rules. Here the
first husband has a special position as the father, in a sense, of *all*
the children. His is a ritual marriage, and at his death all the
children observe the customs connected with the Indian belief
that the bereaved are for a time in a state of religious impurity.
Subsequent husbands make gifts and pay midwives' expenses.
But the domestic unit consists of a mother, her daughters, and
their children, and for all important purposes descent is counted
exclusively through women.

This is an extreme form of a matrilineal society, where children derive their group affiliations and claim their inheritance
through their mothers. Man and wife do not set up house together: the husband visits his wife who lives with her mother's
family. Among the matrilineal Trobriand Islanders, according
to Malinowski, even the biological role of the father in conception is unknown. This assertion has been much questioned,
part of the evidence against it being the Trobrianders' undoubted
technical knowledge of pig-breeding, and therefore of the role
of the boar. But whether or not the Trobrianders have this
biological knowledge, the role of the father in their society
differs greatly from his role in the primarily patrilineal societies
where a child derives its name, and often its status and inheritance, from its father. Mary Kingsley noted in the matrilineal
society of the Igalwa of the then French Congo that

The father's responsibility, as regards authority over his own children, is very slight. The really responsible male relative is the mother's
elder brother. From him must leave to marry be obtained for either
girl or boy; to him and the mother must the present be taken which
is exacted on the marriage of a girl; and should the mother die, on
him and not on the father lies the responsibility of rearing the
children . . . after his own brothers by the same mother, they become
his heirs. . . .

The matrilineal peoples were once thought to represent a more
'primitive' stage in the evolution of the family than the patrilineal peoples, on the grounds that in a supposedly promiscuous
primitive horde, or in societies at the 'hunting and collecting'

stage, children would necessarily be brought up by their mothers, and cling to them and know them, while the particular father would not be known. There is no historical evidence for this argument, and it will certainly not hold if the supposedly more 'primitive' matrilineal descent is assumed to be associated with a general cultural poverty and simplicity. The matrilineal Nayar, or matrilineal peoples like the Akan of Ghana, Minang-kabau of Sumatra, and even the Plains Indians of North America are by any standards as highly organized socially as many patrilineal peoples and culturally far richer than some.

In writing of patrilineal societies, and following Fustel de Coulanges, anthropologists have used terms borrowed from Roman law to make a very necessary distinction between the man who is socially and legally responsible for a wife's children, and the man who actually begat them. The legal father is the *pater* and socially recognized guardian, and the biological father, the begetter, is the *genitor*.

In modern Western society, the *pater* and the *genitor* are ideally the same person, though even then the legal father of a child may not be what we should call (with our sense of the primacy of biological kinship) the 'real' father. Our 'paternity' suits are often not about paternity in the Roman sense at all, but about who was the begetter, the *genitor*, of a child. Amongst some peoples this question would be less significant than among ourselves, for the *pater* and *genitor* are quite often different persons. A Dinka husband may depute a kinsman to sleep with his wife if for some reason or another he cannot himself fill the complete role of husband, provided always that he may claim the children. He is *pater*, his kinsman *genitor*. A widow may sometimes be allowed to choose her own lover, when it is clearly recognized that any children born of this union are the legal children of the man in whose name cattle were originally given for her in marriage. The maxim of Roman law which asserts that 'the father (*pater*) is he who can show that he married the mother' applies in many societies today.

The fact that a woman is the wife of a particular man, and therefore that her children born after the union are indisputably his children and members of his group in the eyes of the society, is commonly established by a substantial payment or gift from the bridegroom and his family to the family of the bride. The type of wealth handed over in marriage varies greatly from society to society. Money, hoes and spears, livestock, trade goods, beads are but a few of the items, and in some cases service may be rendered for this purpose, as when Jacob served for Rachel. A bride may also be expected to bring with her a dowry, or an exchange gift may be made by the family of the bride to that of the groom.

Europeans often misunderstood the giving of bridewealth as the purchasing of women, and it was particularly disapproved of by many of the early missionaries in Africa. Not all of these however were of one mind. A comprehensive work on marriage and related topics, *Survey of African Marriage and Family Life* (ed. Arthur Phillips, 1953), quotes the American missionary to the Zulu, Daniel Lindley, who in the 1860's took a more sociological view of native marriage custom than many of his contemporaries, and saw virtues in it:

Why is it that I have not heard of six illegitimate children since I came among these people? Why is it that wives are required to be true and faithful to their husbands? Why is it that wives are not daily driven off and new ones taken?

Because, he thought, of native marriage custom.

Every year more husbands are separated by the law of Connecticut than I have heard of here in 33 years, where men can divorce their wives by word of mouth. . . . Why is it that family organization here is as perfect as it could be made with the existence of polygamy? There is seldom a dispute among children about the division of a man's property, however many wives he may have had.

As Lindley recognized, in most traditional societies marriage is something more than a union of two individuals or even of their immediate families. It involves relationships between whole groups of people, so that any marriage has something of the wider social significance of the few dynastic or otherwise politically significant marriages of modern Western society, and marriage alliances and affinal relationships are of great importance.

'Kinship', indeed, is considered by modern anthropologists in terms of descent and marriage alliance. Whole descent-groups are linked by past marriages, and from the point of view of any individual, one very significant division of kin is that between the lineage of the husband and father and the lineage of the wife and mother, a distinction preserved only to a slight extent in our own seating of the bride's and bridegroom's families and friends on opposite sides of the church, and in our now almost archaic expressions the 'spear side' and 'distaff side'. Louis Dumont has shown that over much of South India the principle of marriage alliance, and relationships of affinity, are even more important for an understanding of kinship nomenclature and behaviour than the principle of common descent, for both matrilineal and patrilineal peoples have in common a single basic pattern of marriage rules and ceremonies. Again, among the Azande of the Sudan, according to Major P. M. Larken

... relationship by marriage imposes on the families of both parties the duty of mutual help and support to an even greater degree than does blood relationship. Therefore, the greater the number of families he allies himself to, by marriage with one of their members, the stronger is his position in society, for he will have them at his back in all his doings. On the other hand, his fathers-in-law probably expect from him more than he from them, for it is they who are the conferrers of the benefit, in allowing him to marry their daughters.

There sometimes appears a suggestion of reluctance to part with daughters in marriage, especially in rich and powerful families. The daughters of a Shilluk king are not permitted to marry at all. Marriage ceremonies may also include more or less stylized displays of hostility between the bride's and bridegroom's parties, since marriage here creates an alliance between groups who have been potential enemies. There may be a show of removing the bride by force from her people, in customs, perhaps like carrying the bride across the threshold, which were at one time interpreted as survivals of an older form of marriage by capture, when all brides, it was supposed, had to be abducted.

Personal choice of marriage partner sometimes, even often, gives way to other important considerations of practical, economic, and political suitability. Not that affection, or even love in the modern romantic sense are necessarily absent, but they cannot initially play the predominant part that they have come to play in modern Europe and America. The primary end of marriage is often not 'companionship' or sexual pleasure but the birth of legitimate children, and it has frequently been observed that spinsters or bachelors of marriageable age are very rare indeed in most 'primitive' societies.

Where bridewealth is given in traditional circumstances, the goods required often cannot be provided by a single individual or by his immediate family. Consequently a wide range of kin are required to help one of their members obtain a wife, and those who received bridewealth from the marriage of one of their daughters are similarly obliged to distribute it widely amongst those who have helped them in getting wives for their sons. In such complicated indebtedness, very many people are necessarily interested in any particular marriage, and in the total process of the collection and distribution of bridewealth, several marriages may be dependent on each other. In litigation over marriages, the details of many payments and exchanges over two generations may well be recalled at length by all the disputants.

An extreme example of the implications of marriage debts is found among the Anuak of Ethiopia and the Sudan, who marry for comparatively scarce necklaces of small blue beads, *dimui*, and old spearheads, as well as the occasional rifle and small numbers of stock. The beads and spearheads are ancient and of unknown origin. They cannot be counterfeited, nor can new supplies be obtained, and from loss or accidental destruction the total stock of acceptable bridewealth has therefore diminished over the years. Meanwhile the acceptable quantity required for a good marriage has not been significantly reduced.

Consequently it often happens that a man must borrow necklaces to marry with, which have been made available through a series of previous marriages. If one of the earlier marriages breaks up, and the bride's family must therefore return the necklaces, they may have to ask for them back from the man who next used them, and he will have to return *his* wife to her people in order to redeem them. If meanwhile they have been used again, still another marriage may have to be dissolved. One divorce can thus necessitate several more. Marriage itself has become subject to a kind of inflation, since more marriages are contracted than there is bridewealth available to under-write them. This could not occur where stock of some kind, which reproduce themselves, were used for bridewealth.

Bridewealth then usually engages the interests of large num-bers of people in any particular marriage, and along with the lavish feasts and elaborate ceremonies frequently accompanying a wedding, serves as a public demonstration of the legality of a union and the legitimacy of its issue. In patrilineal societies more particularly, the payment of bridewealth marks the trans-fer of rights in a woman's services, domestic, sexual, and pro-creative, from one group to another, and is regarded as a com-pensation to the girl's family for the loss of a daughter whom they have had the labour and expense of rearing and teaching.

Claude Lévi-Strauss, whose *Les Structures Elémentaires de la Parenté* (1949) is the most substantial theoretical work on kin-ship since L. H. Morgan's in the last century, has specially emphasized the principles of reciprocity and exchange as they appear in the marriage rules of many different societies. The giving of bridewealth for wives is one, and the most common, form of exchange, but a direct exchange of daughters may be arranged between exogamous groups. The Tiv of Nigeria are reported to have sometimes given daughter for daughter in marriage between two families. Each of these daughters, be-coming a wife in her new home, took the name of the daughter for whom she had been exchanged—an indication that they were regarded as substitutes for each other.

Here exchange of girls may have been conducted more or less haphazardly between families who had reached agreement upon it, but in many cases whole societies are divided into a fixed number of groups or classes for purposes of marriage. The simplest form of this would occur if a society were to consist simply of two groups, or moieties, within each of which marriage was forbidden. Group A would therefore have to ex-change its girls with Group B. Where the number of fixed intermarrying groups is larger, more complex rules determine

the range of marriage choices. Group A may give girls to
Group B, but receive them from Group C, which in turn re-
ceives them from B and so on. The Australian aborigines are
noted for various systems of marriage rules based upon the
division of their tribes into a number of marriage classes. An
early description of one such kind of division is given in an
account (1889) of an escaped convict, William Buckley, who
lived for thirty-two years among Australian aborigines who

. . . never under any circumstances married blood relations. Indeed,
such an idea would have been regarded with an indignation amount-
ing almost to horror. And to prevent the slightest probability of a
black committing such a heinous crime, in their eyes, they had a
system of dividing their tribes into classes. All people of one class
were counted as being connected by blood, and, therefore, could not
intermarry. Thus a man could not marry a woman belonging to his
father's or his mother's class.

More complex systems than this with more numerous 'classes'
have been discovered, some of them still subjects of contro-
versy. These studies are now highly specialized, and Rodney
Needham, an authority in them has greatly helped me by
writing:

In the last quarter of the nineteenth century the study of what was
taken to be 'group marriage' in Australia brought into prominence
an institution which Durkheim named 'connubium' and has more
recently been termed *prescriptive alliance*. This designation refers to
relationship terminologies which prescribe marriage with a certain
category of woman, and to the fact that lineal descent groups are
brought into alliance by the application of this categorical prescription. Typically, all the members of a society practising prescriptive alliance are reckoned as relatives, and the terminology distin-
guishes these exhaustively as either lineal kin or as affines. For example, all the women of a man's own generation may be distinguished simply as 'sister' (prohibited woman) or as 'wife' (potential
spouse, permitted woman, etc.). (It was partly the classificatory
application of terms translated as 'husband' and 'wife' to men and
women of distinct groups which induced European observers to infer that all the women of one group were married to all the men of
another, and thus to speak of 'group marriage'.)

As Lévi-Strauss has shown, there are two main forms of prescriptive alliance: symmetric and asymmetric. The former comprises the so-called section-systems (with two, four, or eight sections), and is characterized by a reciprocal exchange of women, by bilateral cross-cousin (see p. 104) marriage, and associated prestations [gifts] between lineal descent groups. The latter is represented only by the system prescribing marriage with the matrilateral[1] cross-cousin and prohibiting the patrilateral[2] cross-cousin: in such a society there can be no reciprocal exchange between alliance groups, but women and other prestations are transferred unilaterally in such a way as to 'circulate' throughout the society.

Two-section systems have been found in very many parts of the world, notably in the Pacific and in South America; four- and eight-section systems are confined to Australia; asymmetric alliance is typically found in northern Burma and in eastern Indonesia, but occurs also in Siberia, Bolivia, and other areas. No prescriptive alliance system based on marriage with the patrilateral cross-cousin has yet been reliably reported, and it has been argued that such a system is impossible.

A feature of special interest in prescriptive alliance systems is that characteristically there is so close a structural concordance between social structure and cosmological notions that they may be analysed together as aspects of one and the same classification, social and symbolic.

We see then how very far from the truth were those Victorian writers who assumed that peoples with the simplest and crudest material culture would be lacking in definite marital institutions, and near to complete sexual promiscuity.

Strictly monogamous marriage and the elementary or conjugal family of husband, wife, and children—the 'natural' family of European moral theology—living together in their separate household, are thus very specialized forms of these institutions. Notions of family and household have more usually included larger and more elaborately organized groups and relationships of kin and affines. Two instances from different continents will show something of their variety of form.

The family amongst the Hindus, for instance, is assumed by

---

[1] i.e. on the mother's side.   [2] i.e. on the father's side.

law and custom to be a 'joint family'. This means that all males have equal rights in the property of the family simply by virtue of being born into it. All women, which includes the unmarried girls and those who have married in from other joint families, have a right to maintenance. Legally the senior member (father or eldest brother) is only the manager of the family property and he may not without the consent of his 'coparceners', as the *male* members are called, alienate any of the family's property. The married sons with their wives and children live in the joint household and eating food cooked at a common hearth expresses their jointness. The girls of the family will have their marriage expenses paid from the joint property. Although formal Hindu law recognizes the right of any coparcener to sue for a division when he wants it, this rarely takes place in the lifetime of the father. Indeed, in rural areas, it is not uncommon to find groups which have remained joint for several generations. Even when a division does take place, either as a matter of convenience or as the result of a quarrel, the larger joint family breaks up into small joint families which in their turn will expand. It does not, even today, break up into the non-expandable units as it would in our own society.

A different example is an African polygamous or more strictly, polygynous, household. There each wife has her own hut and looks after her own children. Families there are united in the father and divided through the mothers, though there may be much sharing of tasks among wives. In fact many or even most people in a polygynous society may have only one wife, since a plurality of wives involves expenditure which none but the fairly rich can afford. Nevertheless the polygynous household remains an ideal, and it was almost a necessity for chiefs and other persons of importance who were required to do much entertaining. It offers the hope of numerous offspring and wide alliances, and alleviates for husbands the widespread African prohibition of sexual intercourse with a wife during the period—often two years or so—when she is suckling a child.

Even those couples who are effectively monogamous are not likely to live alone with their children. There are few African

households, at least in villages, which do not include other kin
more or less permanently domiciled there. From their earliest
years small children brought up in these circumstances command the attentions of a wider group of kin than most urban
or suburban children, and have to learn traditional ways of
placing these kin in relation to themselves and to each
other.

Many anthropological studies, of which Margaret Mead's
Growing up in New Guinea (1931) and *Coming of Age in Samoa*
(1929) were pioneering popular works, have dealt with the
implications of such different forms of upbringing for the
moulding of the personality of individuals and the problems of
social adjustment. They have asked, and tried to answer, such
questions as why it is that in some societies violence is much
rarer than in others, or why the problems of adolescence about
which Western society now hears so much, do not seem to be
by any means universal.

The very varied forms of marriage, family, and household,
and the strong emphasis upon social as distinct from simply
biological definitions of kinship, have been accompanied by
many systems of naming and classifying kin very different from
those to which we have become accustomed. For an anthropologist, one of the first steps towards an understanding of kinship
is the collection and analysis of the terminology used for kin
of different categories. Probably the first European writer to
draw attention to families and kin-groups much wider in range
than any found in Europe, and to attempt some comparison
of them, was a Jesuit, P. Lafitau, in his *Mœurs des Sauvages
Amériquains Comparées aux Mœurs des Premiers Temps*, published
in 1724.

Lafitau had found among the Iroquois and other Indians of
North America ways of classifying kin which he thought comparable in principle with those known among the ancient
Hebrews, Chaldeans, and Egyptians. A central feature of the
Amerindian usage was that brothers and sisters were not distinguished as a group from their cousins in the way we distinguish them. The children of sisters and the children of
brothers regarded each other as 'brothers' and 'sisters'. But the

children of a brother and his sister regarded each other, according to Lafitau, as 'cousins', not as brothers and sisters.

'Siblings' is a convenient anthropological term for referring equally to brothers and sisters. The children of two brothers or two sisters—that is, of siblings of the same sex—are called 'parallel cousins', while the children of a brother and a sister —of siblings of different sexes—are 'cross-cousins'. So in the specialized vocabulary necessarily used by anthropologists discussing the kinship systems, one might say that according to Lafitau among the Iroquois parallel cousins were referred to by the same terms as those used for brothers and sisters, but cross-cousins were referred to by quite different terms. This distinction between parallel and cross-cousins is an important one in many other societies. Marriage may be encouraged or even prescribed between cousins of one sort, and totally forbidden between cousins of the other. Among some of the Swahili of East Africa, the most desirable choice in marriage that a man can make is the daughter of his father's sister or of his mother's brother—that is, one of his cross-cousins. Marriage with the daughter of the father's brother, or of the mother's sister—that is, with parallel cousins—is forbidden. It is to be expected therefore that the terms used for these two types of cousin, and the approved pattern of social relation with them, should be quite different. This is only a simple example of the intricately varied sets of relations between cousins of different degrees, who in English kinship terminology tend to be classified together since it is usually not important socially to distinguish between them.

What Lafitau had actually recognized was that his Indians had no words for 'brother' and 'sister' which would exactly designate just those kin to whom the words refer in our own usage. So all those who called each other 'brother' and 'sister'—or rather, by the native terms for which 'brother' and 'sister' might be made to serve as translations—were by no means brothers and sisters in our sense. He had begun to do what every anthropological student of kinship has had to do since—to take the native kinship terminology as a guide to the classification of kin and a pointer to significant social relationships, and to distinguish between actual biological relationship on the one hand, and on the other, the conventions of custom and language which determine what *social* meaning is given to the basic biological facts of mating and procreation. So, having observed that Iroquois 'brothers' and 'sisters' were not really all the children of the same parents, he found it 'easy to conceive how the Egyptians, and several other peoples, could marry their sisters, that is, their first cousins or even relatives of a more distant degree', thus making the reports of royal incest appear less unnatural. More important for his own religious interests, his discussion of such extended uses of terms of relationship which in Europe referred to narrower ranges of kin enabled him to comment on a detail of St Mark's Gospel, where

The cousins of the Saviour, in a quite distant degree, are called his brothers, which has led the heretics to say that St Joseph had other children, either by some other wife, or by the Blessed Virgin herself. The general rule of the Jews was to call each other brothers and sisters, in whatever degree of relationship they were in collateral lines, when they could trace their ancestry back on both sides to the same origin [*la souche*].

In the last century L. H. Morgan, whose work on the Iroquois and evolutionary interpretations of different forms of marriage and family, have already been mentioned (Chap. 1, pp. 12–14) made comprehensive comparative studies of the wide-range kinship which had interested Lafitau, and, it is claimed, without knowledge of the latter's observations. Morgan introduced the term 'classificatory' for systems of kinship nomenclature in which large numbers of kin are categorized together by the use of a single word for a type of relationship—where for example all men of the mother's clan and generation may be called by a term which might be translated as 'mother's brother'. Lineal relatives (e.g. father, grandfather) and collateral relatives (e.g. what we should call uncle, great-uncle) were here subsumed under the same term. This classificatory kinship he opposed to what he called 'descriptive' systems of referring to kin, in which terms were used with more limited and specific application to particular persons.

Like many of his contemporaries, Morgan sometimes exaggerated differences between 'primitive' usage and that of his own society. W. H. R. Rivers, whose *Kinship and Social Organization* (1913) appraises Morgan's work and tries to advance theoretically from it, noting objections to the use of the term 'classificatory':

... on the ground that our own terms of relationship also apply to classes of persons the term 'brother', for instance, to all male children of the same father and mother, the term 'uncle' to all brothers of the father and mother as well as to the husband of an aunt, while the term 'cousin' may denote a still larger class.

But there still remain very great differences, from society to society, in the range of classificatory terminology and the extent to which it is habitually used, and (in support of Morgan) Rivers continues:

... in the system to which the word 'classificatory' is usually applied, the classificatory principle applies far more widely, and in some cases even more logically and consistently. In the most complete form of the classificatory system there is not one single term of relationship the use of which tells us that reference is being made to one person only, whereas in our own system there are six such terms, viz., husband, wife, father, mother, father-in-law and mother-in-law. In those systems in which the classificatory principle is carried to its extreme degree every term is applied to a class of persons.

The logical and social implications of different systems of classifying kin have been examined in much highly specialized and technical anthropological writing. In the nature of the material the diagrammatic representation of kin-relationships produces very complicated charts which Malinowski impatiently referred to as 'kinship algebra'. But if it be assumed that the kinship nomenclature of any society is not purely random, it is reasonable to inquire into its internal consistency and to seek reasons for it.

Our own use of the same terms 'uncle' and 'aunt' for certain categories of relatives whether they are on the father's or the mother's side, suggests what we know to be true on other grounds—that it is on the whole unimportant for us, in speaking of or to these relatives, to make a sharp distinction between the brothers and sisters of the father and those of the mother. Such a usage would appear very strange to many peoples who, like the Arabs, differentiate very strictly between maternal and paternal uncles and aunts, and use quite different words and associations for them.

Similarly, for anyone taking for granted the English system of classifying kin as represented in English kinship nomenclature, other systems which use the same term for grandparents or certain grandparents, and grandchildren, must appear anomalous. Rivers himself found on the island of Pentecost in the New Hebrides that the wife's mother was designated by the same term as the daughter, in a system which he found 'to have so bizarre and complex a character that I could hardly believe at first it could be other than the result of a ludicrous misunderstanding between myself and my seemingly intelligent and trustworthy informants'. He had found other cases in which features of classificatory kinship terminology could be explained by particular marriage rules, and in this case eventually came actually to believe the implausible proposition that this New Hebridean system, which classified a grandmother with a granddaughter, might be explained by habitual marriages between a grandfather and his granddaughter. 'Grandmother' and 'granddaughter' would then come to the same thing.

The particular connexions of systems of kinship terminology with marriage rules and other local details of social structure and customary behaviour can only be demonstrated by minute investigation in particular societies; but, in general, the prevalance of extensive classificatory systems in primitive or traditional societies indicates that for them the idiom and attitudes of kinship are far more important over a wider range of social relations, than in societies of the modern Western type.

We have only faint parallels to this use of kinship terms outside the immediate family circle. One is in the way that friends of parents, and of more or less the parents' generation, may become 'courtesy' uncles and aunts. Our avuncular relationship, on whichever side of the family, is associated with advice, indulgence, and affection of a playful kind, and it is consistent with this that those who entertain children on the wireless or in the columns of newspapers tend to adopt the role of uncle or aunt. It would be inconsistent with this role if they were to appear as 'grandparents', who represent a different ideal relationship, and even more were they to usurp the role—for it would be seen as usurpation—of father or mother.

But the kinship behaviour of peoples for whom kinship remains an important principle of social organization is, of course, much more highly formalized, obligatory, and diversified according to persons and their various kinship categories and roles, than that of modern societies. It would be regarded as an unfriendly gesture, among many peoples, not to use the appropriate term of relationship in saluting a remote kinsman, and, by the use of a particular term, a man shows that he expects from him to whom it is addressed a part, at least, of the approved behaviour associated with all kin of that category. So 'my mother's brother' even if he be really a very distant clansman of the mother who has rarely been seen, is expected to some extent to behave like the mother's own brother, and has a right to expect his 'nephews' to behave towards him according to that status.

This is clearly important when the roles of different kinds of kin are clearly defined, and appropriate behaviour to kinsmen and affines forms a large part of etiquette, morality, and religion. The 'mother's brother', to use this instance, is often regarded in patrilineal societies as the uncle with whom specially affectionate and familiar relations are maintained, in contrast to the 'father's brother', in relations with whom constraint and respect are conventionally prescribed, and with whom conflict over inheritance or the exercise of authority is more likely to arise. A father's brother, and even more a father's half-brother, but not a mother's brother, may here be the wicked uncle who figures in our children's stories, but no longer in our social life.

Other common rules are that certain relatives—particularly men and their mothers-in-law—should avoid each other, and that others are permitted, and may be required, to exchange insults in a jesting way. A. R. Radcliffe-Brown's examination of these 'joking relationships' (in *Structure and Function in Primitive Society*, 1952) is an attempt to relate and explain 'in general and abstract terms' these customs of avoidance and respect on the one side, and of licensed familiarity on the other. His view is that both joking and avoidance occur in situations where important common interests are accompanied by the potentiality of conflict: 'The alliance by extreme respect, by partial or complete avoidance, prevents such conflict but keeps the parties conjoined. The alliance by joking does the same thing in a different way.' Underlying 'joking relationships' also, though, is of course the common human capacity to be entertained by outrageousness. In one of the first accounts of Africa by an African to be edited and produced in a really scholarly way (*Akiga's Story*, translated and annotated by Rupert East, 1939) the author, a Tiv of Nigeria, writes:

The first word a child learns is *de* (don't!) and after that *taata* and *nam* (give me). Then he learns swear-words like *iaw!* (dog). When he says this his mother laughs delightedly, and calls someone to hear what a clever child she has got; he can swear like anything! 'Swear at him!' she says. The child does so, and everyone is amused. The mother teaches him some more, and he grows up with a good stock of swear-words.

A privileged offensiveness, as among ourselves sometimes, amuses.

Apart from classificatory kinship terminologies, though often closely associated with the use of them, are other ways of placing kin in significant social categories. One common distinction is that made by the Romans, but also by the Nuer and others at the present day, between cognatic and agnatic relationship. Cognatic kin are all those to whom a person is related by descent either through the mother or the father. Agnatic kin are those to whom he is related, by descent counted exclusively through men from a common ancestor who may be placed many generations away in the past. It is quite usual for this agnatic descent to be remembered to ten to fifteen generations or more, though there is good reason to believe that many such long genealogies are partly fictitious. Ancestors who are not significant for explaining the relationships between the living tend to be forgotten, while in an oral tradition generations are telescoped, and ancestors displaced. Consequently an oral genealogy cannot be safely used, by itself, as a basis for historical reconstruction, or we should have to believe that some peoples first appeared in the world only a few generations ago, in the time of their first named ancestors.

Where descent groups are important social units, there is a tendency in many situations to place more emphasis upon the clan or lineage than upon the individual families which are united in it. The continuity of the lineage is regarded as ultimately and religiously significant; individual members and their families are the means by which new members are born into it. This is not to say that the ordinary family affections of modern societies are weaker or are absent. Only in addition to these, there are attachments to the wider descent group, as any member looks back to his ancestors, and forward to generations of progeny who, together, over the years, form a society of the living and the dead. Many Africans thus preferred to join their ancestors in the Hell preached by missionaries, than be divided from them in the Heaven.

This philosophy is often accompanied by customs which ensure that a member of the lineage who dies childless shall not lose his position as a link in the chain of ancestry. In the institution of the levirate, a man is required to take the wife of his dead brother, and raise children to his name, as was demanded of the ancient Jews in the Book of Deuteronomy:

If brethren dwell together, and one of them die, and have no child, the wife of the dead shall not marry without unto a stranger; her husband's brother shall go in to her, and take her to him to wife, and perform the duty of an husband's brother unto her. And it shall be that the first-born which she beareth shall succeed in the name of his brother which is dead, that his name be not put out of Israel.

The levirate, and the 'sororate' in which a dead wife is replaced by her sister, also preserve the stability of existing relations between families whose members have married, and a considerable problem is raised for Christian missionaries, who must forbid the levirate while at the same time being seriously concerned with provision for widows which in its way the levirate ensures. Less common than the levirate, and expressing in an extreme form the necessity of preserving the line of descent, is what has been called 'ghost' marriage, when a girl is legally married, with the payment of bridewealth, to a dead man, to whose name she bears children by someone chosen to cohabit with her.

These customs emphasize the difference between *pater* and *genitor*, the social and biological father earlier discussed, and indicate a conception of 'the family' much broader than our own, in which the dead and those as yet unborn are intimately linked together in the minds of the living, as an Arabic word for a line of spiritual descent, *silsila*, 'chain', suggests. An African image for the development of the lineage over generations, despite the death of its individual members and dissolution of their families, is drawn from the growth and branching of a tree, or the habit of growth of the gourd. The plant grows from the seed of a gourd, and its runners spread out from the parent plant. The runners produce gourds, which in turn seed where they have grown and continue the process of spreading and proliferation. Each plant dies, but every new plant has an essential, invisible connexion, through all those which have produced it, with the original seed.

Concern for ancestry and generation is shown in the filial piety, the cults of ancestors and the prayers for fertility which have widely played a central part in religious practice. Cults of the dead are not for the dead alone. They represent a religious commitment to the welfare of the groups to which the dead still belong, and that welfare is assured by the fertility and vitality of the living. Kinship is not only a cardinal principle of primitive legal, political, and economic relations; it helps to determine judgements of morality, and at a still deeper level relates intimately to religious belief.

This religious element in the relations between kin is not seen only in the prayer offerings and sacrifices made to the ancestral or totemic spirits which with the well-being of various kin-groups are thought to be associated. At the very foundation of any family, and therefore of all the many different forms of organized relationship between persons as members of families —at the basis of any kinship system, that is—is a religious prohibition, the prohibition of incest.

The degrees and classes of kin between whom marriage is forbidden, and sexual intercourse discouraged or proscribed, vary immensely from society to society. They cannot be regarded simply as different ways of avoiding the supposed physical consequences of inbreeding; for, first, many peoples do not so explain them, and second, because they often do not depend strictly upon the degree of blood relationship, as when parallel-cousin marriage is prohibited but cross-cousin marriage encouraged. Again, marriage is forbidden between certain categories of biologically unrelated persons, as between those who have been suckled at the same breast or, in Christianity, between godparents and their godchildren or (a *cause célèbre* of Victorian England) between a man and his deceased wife's sister.

In all societies, to ignore incest prohibitions is a grave sin, and one thought not only to endanger the guilty couple but to subvert the social order and involve the whole group in a risk of divine retribution. Incest prohibitions, and the various rules of exogamy which determine the range and size of the group within which marriage is forbidden, in practice necessitate a constant widening of social relations. Each family, or larger exogamous unit, depends upon the wives it must obtain from outside for its continuance. A precondition of human society is the union and interdependence of such exogamous units, a union created by marriages and hence by marriage regulations. Claude Lévi-Strauss has expressed in an essay in *Man, Culture and Society* (ed. Shapiro, 1956) a sociological view of the significance of incest prohibitions in observing that 'if social organization had a beginning' (considering man, that is, at once evolving from an animal state):

... this could only have consisted in the incest prohibition, since ... the incest prohibition is, in fact, a kind of remodelling of the biological conditions of mating and procreation which know no rule, as can be seen from observing animal life, compelling them to become perpetuated only in an artificial framework of taboos and obligations. It is there, and only there, that we find a passage from nature to culture, from animal to human life, and that we are in a position to understand the very essence of their articulation.

In the field of psycho-analysis, Freud considered similar problems, though his use of anthropological material in *Totem and Taboo* leaves much to be desired.

Incest may be regarded then as the essentially anti-social act. It denies the necessity of the wider social group, and tends to abolish fundamental distinctions between man and the lower animals, distinctions which are explicitly valued perhaps particularly by peoples for whom the preservation of their specifically human culture involves hard and constant struggle against natural circumstances.

In *Ritual and Belief in Morocco*, Edward Westermarck tells several Moroccan stories which represent a recognition that by disregard of human social regulations man loses his humanity. The wild boar, for example, is said once to have been a teacher of canon law, who merely laughed at his pupils when they threw their food at each other instead of eating it. An angel then called to him, 'O wild boar, tell your monkeys that they should let alone the food given by God,' and the teacher became a boar and his pupils monkeys. It is also believed (and this is not confined to the Moroccans) that the monkey was a man who was transformed for committing an offence. Westermarck records, as reasons for this punishment, that the monkey committed incest with his sister, or had sexual intercourse in daytime in the month of Ramadan, or he urinated in milk, washed his face with it, and cleaned himself with bread after defecating.

Incest is there listed with offences which result in the loss of human status, and destroy human and divine order. It is a denial of all the values of kinship in that it represents (what the Chinese character for incest literally means) 'confusion of relationships'. As such it is not only a serious social misdemeanour in the sphere of kinship, but also a sin, a rejection of a supposedly basic moral order, a disregard for the limits supposed to be ordained for human behaviour. It is these which religious and cognate beliefs have been particularly concerned with.

6
Belief and Knowledge

We have imprisoned our own conceptions, by the lines
which we have drawn in order to exclude the conceptions
of others.

S. T. Coleridge, *Biographia Literaria*

CONFLICT BETWEEN RELIGION AND NATURAL SCIENCE,
concerning the origin and status of Man, disturbed many
scholars of the last century not only intellectually but also in
their personal lives. Charles Darwin, who had originally intended to become a clergyman of the Established Church, recalled that even when an undergraduate he did not 'in the least
doubt the strict and literal truth of every word in the Bible'. Sir
James Frazer had been brought up in a devout and affectionate
Presbyterian family, where he had 'learned the Shorter Cate-
chism by heart and accepted its teaching without question as the
standard of orthodoxy'. Like so many others of the time, both
of them came to reject the doctrines in which they had been
reared, which were too narrow, or too narrowly understood, to
accommodate their mature experience.

Even the religion of educated Europeans of their own class
was thus associated for them as for others like them with an
immaturity of sentiment and reason, a timid or obstinate tradi-
tionalism, which they had personally outgrown. Still more compounded of error and misunderstanding, arising from false
analogical reasoning, and ignorance of natural causes, laws, and
processes, therefore appeared the religion of uneducated, un-

scientific peoples who were assumed to have remained closer to an original psychological infancy of mankind.

Tylor's theory of the basis of religion, and Frazer's of the nature of magic, illustrate the approach of many Victorian writers to these topics. I have already mentioned (Chap. 1, p. 8) Tylor's minimal definition of religion as 'a belief in spiritual beings'. This simplest form of religion, 'animism' as he called it, arose, he thought ,when primitive peoples had reflected upon their experience of immaterial forms in dreams, or considered the difference between a living man and his corpse. Primitive Man, considering these mysteries and anxious for an explanation, would infer the existence of a human soul, immaterial and separable from the body. From this he would develop the idea of other souls and spirits 'from the tiniest elf that sports in the long grass up to the heavenly Creator and Ruler of the world, the Great Spirit'.

According to one of Frazer's most influential theories, magical practices were to be explained by a 'law of sympathy' governing primitive thought. From this 'law' followed such common beliefs as that gold might be used to cure jaundice, or that a person might be injured by the magical treatment of his nail- or hair-clippings. Things which had a striking quality in common, like the yellowness of gold and jaundice, or which had once been in intimate contact, were believed to affect one another. This is, of course, a true account of common beliefs, and Frazer's categories of 'imitative' and 'contagious' magic still have some value; but he was too ready to regard this descriptive formulation as a conclusion to his investigation.

For Tylor and more particularly Frazer, primitive religion and magic were erroneous means towards a knowledge and control of human circumstance, and particularly of the physical world which in their day men of science had really begun to achieve by rational methods. In France, the more philosophical Lévy-Bruhl posited a primitive mentality quite different in orientation from that of modern philosophers and scientists, a synthesizing, affective, poetic mentality which neither made, nor aimed at making, the distinctions of European logic. In primitive thought, men and natural beings and objects might 'participate' mystically in one another's existence, as when among people who hold totemic beliefs a man and his totemic animal are supposed in some sense to share a common life.

Early inquiry into such matters, particularly in Britain, much oversimplified the problems of translation and interpretation of exotic ideas and customs. Original texts from native informants were very few. The scholars who claimed to understand 'primitive mentality' knew nothing of the languages in which it was expressed, and had no intimate experience of the actual social and physical conditions of the peoples whose beliefs they confidently interpreted. Consequently much of their interpretation was the result of simple introspection, of supposing themselves in foreign circumstances and imagining how they themselves would then think and act.

Yet the Victorian anthropologists had at least begun seriously to collect and sift evidence about the beliefs of remote cultures which were often absurdly misunderstood by other educated men. They were prepared to compare, as well as contrast, 'savages' with themselves, and they tried to understand some principles of symbolic thought and action on a wide comparative basis. If for them the primitive gods, and possibly all gods, were products of a more or less uninstructed human reason and imagination, they were still examples of 'gods' to be studied, and not 'idols', 'devils', or mere mumbo-jumbo, as they were sometimes made to appear by those who viewed them entirely from the standpoint of their own absolute revealed religious orthodoxies. When a traveller as influential as Sir Samuel Baker could tell the Ethnological Society of London (in 1866) that the Dinka and Shilluk of the Upper Nile had no religion 'nor is the darkness of their minds enlightened by even a ray of superstition', it was as well to have a Tylor to rebuke his opinionated ignorance.

Further, perhaps partly because some of them had themselves exchanged one framework of convictions for another in moving outside religious faiths they had once professed, anthropologists had begun to explore how far truths and beliefs, which seemed self-evidently and absolutely valid to those nurtured in

them, were actually contingent upon particular social and historical circumstances.

Here the French sociologists of the *Année Sociologique*—
Durkheim, Mauss, Hubert and others—were more systematic,
and conscious of their aims, than their British or American
counterparts, who gave less thought to the difference between
sociological and psychological generalizations. For Frazer and
others, the explanation of religious and magical beliefs and
customs lay ultimately in the working of the individual human
mind; and they readily assumed that their own minds were
sufficiently representative of 'the human mind', if at its most
subtle and efficient. The French, more sociologically, insisted
that the very possibilities of thought and experience were given
in a social tradition, which its bearers inherited rather than
chose.

There were thus distinctively *collective* ideas and modes of
behaviour which moulded the individual mind and conscience
differently in different societies. As Durkheim wrote:

... there is in every society a certain group of phenomena which may
be differentiated from those studied by the other natural sciences.
When I fulfil my obligations as brother, husband, or citizen, when I
execute my contracts, I perform duties which are defined, externally
to myself and my acts, in law and custom. Even if they conform to
my own sentiments, and I feel their reality subjectively, such reality
is still objective, for I did not create them; I merely inherited them
through my education. ...

Similarly the church member finds the beliefs and practices of his
religious life ready-made at birth; their existence prior to his own
implies their existence outside himself. ...

From such theoretical starting-points, these French writers
proposed a sociology of ideas and beliefs in which such seemingly fundamental and intuitive notions as those of time, of
space, and of classification were examined in relation to social
conditions.

Anthropological insistence upon the necessity of interpreting
belief and custom as relative to social circumstances has sometimes laid the subject open to charges of a total relativism.
Logically, such a relativism would bring the validity of anthro-

pological findings themselves into question, for if all expressions of 'truth' were *merely* relative to social conditions, then there would be nothing to choose between, say, an anthropologist's interpretation of witchcraft and that of a witch.

But a sociology of ideas and convictions does not necessarily imply that the sociologist himself makes no critical judgement as to their greater or lesser validity. He maintains only that no informed judgement can properly be made unless the notions under consideration are first seen as part of the whole social situation which defines their meaning. Thus, to refer to an earlier example, the giving of bridewealth in marriage might appear superficially to resemble purchase of women, but on closer inspection is seen to be a different kind of transaction. Whether that transaction is commendable, is a question of a different order.

In this concern for the detailed social context, social anthropology in this century seems to have developed in a way parallel to some historical and literary studies (one thinks at random of Collingwood, Namier, Beljame, Q. D. Leavis, L. C. Knights), though professional scholars in these other subjects not unnaturally tend to judge it still by the earlier writings which first made an impact on the cultivated reader. In the first chapter of his work *The Greeks and their Gods* (1950) W. K. C. Guthrie, for example, has given a judicious criticism of the eclecticism of earlier anthropological writers in the field of classical studies— Frazer, Jane Harrison, Gilbert Murray—which differs little in principle from that which any living social anthropologist might produce. They tended too easily to interpret details of classical custom in the light of isolated ethnological facts culled from here and there from quite different peoples and circumstances— Australian aborigines, African kingdoms and so forth. But today, any anthropologist trying to understand the religion of his chosen area would accept the principle laid down by Guthrie for his study of the Greeks, that:

... our primary task is to see the religion of Greece in the historical setting of Greek modes of thought and expression, the life of the city state or Boeotian farm, religion as it was affected by the Persian invasion or the Peloponnesian war, above all religion in a small sea-girt country in an East Mediterranean climate.

Modern anthropological works are similarly grounded in the specificity of very local circumstances. Moreover, the anthropologist has usually had the opportunity of directly experiencing these himself, and need not recreate a foreign way of life by the application of an imaginative scholarship to literature.

But the task does not end with an understanding of specific circumstances only. Though social anthropologists no longer select details of beliefs from all over the world, to fit them together in comprehensive theories of the universal characteristics of totemism, ancestor-worship, witchcraft or the like, they still try to reach conclusions which have some relevance for the interpretation of material other than their own. A movement of thought between general themes and specific detail, with the intention of reaching a better understanding of both, is encouraged, in teaching, from the beginning. What this actually involves may be suggested by considering anthropological treatment of notions that seem most conspicuously and self-evidently false to people who have not been brought up to assume their truth—beliefs in witchcraft.

It seems to be generally taken for granted in modern Western society that the complex of beliefs and acts indicated by the word 'witchcraft' arise from superstitious delusion. Yet in the European past, men whose intellectual brilliance is in other respects unquestioned accepted witchcraft as a fact, and belief in it therefore cannot be regarded as utterly incompatible with an educated, critical, and even scientific intelligence. In the *Religio Medici*, Sir Thomas Browne held that those who denied the reality of witchcraft were themselves witches, thus (and in a way characteristic of witchcraft-thought) interpreting arguments against his own belief so as to confirm it. Francis Bacon, who also believed in witchcraft (though perhaps partly because it was more prudent to appear to do so in the time of the intensely witch-conscious King James I), observed that '. . . the act of envy hath something in it of witchcraft, so there is no other cure of envy than the cure of witchcraft, that is, remove the lot as they call it and lay it on another. . . .' Here, the real existence of witchcraft is predicated where most of us, probably, would be inclined to accept first the existence of envy, and regard witchcraft as a set of fears and superstitions stemming from that vice.

European witchcraft notions were commonly fitted into a Christian theological system, so that witches were regarded as in league with the Devil or other evil spirits in the Christian struggle between good and evil, and persecuted for that reason. Margaret Murray and those whom her zealous writings convince, similarly see European witchcraft largely as an opposition by organized adherents of a pagan religion surviving from pre-Christian times to later Christian orthodoxy.

An anthropological interpretation of witchcraft must however take into account ethnological evidence from other societies where the special historical and theological circumstances which gave European witchcraft its particular form do not exist, and here the information from Africa and some of the Indians of North America is particularly rich.

First we have to try to divest the term 'witchcraft' of the confusion of associations which it has in popular thought. It is commonly associated with 'magic', for example; yet there are many who, like Prospero, might properly be called magicians, but who are certainly not witches. Again, the European belief that witches are in communication with evil spirits is not found everywhere, and cannot therefore be said to be an essential feature of all witchcraft.

Witchcraft, basically, entails attributing many of the evils of life to evil in some other persons, who usually by arcane means attack the health and prosperity of their victims. For the sake of clarity, anthropologists have tended to use the term 'witchcraft' to denote primarily a supposed *psychic* art, producing harm which may not even be held to be entirely deliberately planned. In witchcraft so considered, the witch may not himself know what he has done until, having been accused, he is declared guilty by divination, the consultation of oracles, or some other means of 'smelling out' witches.

Then, given his own initial conviction—which he shares

with his accusers—that such baneful influences do emanate from one person to another, and in the often highly suggestible condition induced by the methods of inquiry which have identified him as a witch, he may well admit his guilt. Hence the numerous confessions obtained, whether legalistically as under the courts and tortures of Europe, or by the clairvoyant means of investigation often used in Africa. Confessions then seem to provide further proof of the existence of witches.

This entirely psychic act, 'witchcraft', may be distinguished from 'sorcery', in which there is a conscious and overt intention to injure expressed in the recitation of some malevolent formula or the symbolic use of material means of causing harm In the complex of relationships of hatred and suspicion to which both these words refer, the element of 'witchcraft' as defined above is not empirically observable. It is wholly in the mind and its imaginings, and no proof of this witchcraft that would satisfy a modern court of law could be adduced, though sometimes the presence of a physical substance said to represent it is established by post-mortem. The workings of sorcery on the other hand might be seen and heard if the sorcerer were caught reciting his formula or using his medicines. They can exist therefore outside the mind, even though their real effects are, from a modern point of view, also in the imagination.

Hence, though a modern court of law might not believe that a sorcerer was capable of producing the harm he intended by the means he actually employed, his intention to do so could be demonstrable without his own confession. Courts in Africa today have in such cases adopted something of the attitude of Thomas Hobbes referred to by Parrinder in his short study, *Witchcraft*: 'I think not that their witchcraft [here one might say "sorcery"] is any real power but yet that they are justly punished for the false belief they have that they can do such mischief, joined with their purpose to do it if they can.'

In practice among people who take such matters seriously, this analytic distinction between sorcery and witchcraft is not always clearly drawn and may not be drawn at all. 'Witches' and 'sorcerers' may represent anything from persons who are materially innocent of any offence except that of having incurred suspicion, fear, and enmity, to members of covens of power-seeking occultists, capable in extreme cases (as far as carefully sifted legal evidence can show) of acts of ritual cannibalism.

This very confusion and overlapping of notions, this interplay of imagination and knowledge, confirm beliefs in witchcraft and sorcery. Those who have done no more than glance at a baby which has then fallen sick, or have merely excited distaste for some feature of their physical appearance, or envy for their success, may come to be suspected of vile secret acts of malice. Yet there is some reason for distinguishing analytically between 'witchcraft' and 'sorcery' on the lines indicated. Some peoples do in their own thought make a comparable distinction, and it is one which (as in witchcraft cases tried in modern courts of law) may have practical consequences. And as a matter of general principle, a social anthropologist is required as far as possible to discard the associative thought which *promotes* belief in order to *study* belief, reducing compound experiences and notions as far as possible to constituent elements. No social phenomenon can be adequately studied merely in the language and categories of thought in which the people among whom it is found represent it to themselves.

The effects attributed to witchcraft or sorcery—sickness, misfortune, death—are as real to believers in witchcraft as to sceptics. The 'effects' in themselves raise no anthropological problem. But the causes to which such effects are attributed, and the form of argument by which they are identified as the results of witchcraft, do create a problem of interpretation for those who deny the validity of witchcraft belief.

Professor Michael Polanyi, in *Personal Knowledge* (1957), tried to clarify this problem, basing his argument partly on the rich material from the Azande of the Sudan, and from that detailed and brilliantly analysed ethnographic information has suggested general conclusions about the nature of our belief and knowledge, quite outside the world of Zande witchcraft.

The Azande's beliefs in witchcraft, like those of other peoples, start from the observed facts of misfortune and differential luck; the desire to explain these; and the assumption that the reasons for them are in other people. 'Witchcraft' for Azande is thus a term used to some extent like 'providence' or 'chance' in England; but behind it is a more searching explanatory intention. 'Witchcraft' accounts primarily for the particular manifestations, rather than general characteristics, of human unhappiness.

A Zande who has cultivated his garden to the best of his ability, let us say, following all locally prescribed procedures, has a bad yield because of some pest. He recognizes that it is the pest that has ruined his crop, but he is not content to let the matter rest there. He wants to know why it is *his* particular crop that has failed, when others promise a fine harvest. Brought up to explain misfortune and death, by 'witchcraft', and to believe that witches and other secret enemies may be identified by the consultation of oracles, he turns to the oracles to discover who may be responsible for his bad luck.

Of the several kinds of Zande oracle, the most authoritative is *benge*, a poison administered to chickens whose reactions to it vary and are interpreted as positive or negative answers to questions asked of the poison oracle. A Zande text gives some indication of how this works:

Benge is the wood from which they [Azande] derive oracles. If a man's relative dies he consults *benge* about his death in order to find out the witch who killed him. . . .

A Zande catches some chickens today and takes them to *benge*. He mixes *benge* with a little water and he seizes a chicken and pours *benge* into its beak, and addresses *benge* thus: '*Benge, benge*, you are in the throat of the chicken. I will die this year, *benge* hear it, twist the fowl round and round and lay down its corpse. It is untrue, I will eat my eleusine this year and the year after, let the fowl survive.' If he will not die the fowl survives. If he will die the fowl dies in accordance with the speech of *benge*.

Such beliefs can be shown to have several important functions and effects in Zande society. For instance witchcraft beliefs represent a kind of popular psychology and moral philosophy, since the people whom a Zande expects to bewitch him, and whose names are likely to be put before the oracle, are those whom he thinks have reason to dislike him. These also are likely to be those whom he himself dislikes. To suspect witchcraft, then, is to assess motive and intention. Also (since the wing of a fowl that has died from *benge* in an oracular consultation may be sent to the witch identified by it, to blow upon to 'cool' his witchcraft) the result is to deal openly and frankly with the minor irritations of human relationships before they accumulate into determined hatred. Writing of a very different people, the Navaho Indians of North America, the late Clyde Kluckhohn concluded that

In a society where the relative strength of anticipation of punishment for overt aggression is high, witchcraft allows imaginary aggression. Witchcraft channels the displacement of aggression, facilitating emotional adjustment with a minimum disturbance of social relationships.

therefore also:

Witchcraft belief allows the verbalization of anxiety in a framework that is understandable and that implies the possibility of doing something.

Witches (who are living individuals) are potentially controllable by the society; the caprices of environment are not.

But when all allowance has been made for such positive functions of witchcraft beliefs, it should not be forgotten that the practice may sometimes involve sorcery too—the actual performance of acts of aggression, 'ritual' cannibalism, and the inversion of accepted values which among the Navaho, according to Kluckhohn, are inhibited by being performed in the imagination.

Zande acceptance of witchcraft and oracles has another function more specific to Zande society. When legal cases lie for injury—for witchcraft, adultery, or other wrongs which it is easy to suspect but difficult to prove—and the evidences from different primary consultations of the oracle are contradictory, then the oracles of princes are regarded as final. Thus the regressions of doubt and conflict of opinions in matters which, by their very nature, cannot become clear by demonstrable proofs, have an end in the attribution of infallibility to the oracles of rulers. The princes' oracles then have legal and political functions, in bolstering the system of rule and providing a means of settling issues which must otherwise, to the detriment of effective law, remain in dispute.

Evans-Pritchard emphasized that the Azande were not able or not prepared to put their whole system of beliefs in witch-craft, oracles, and magic to any test which would call the valid-ity of the whole into question. They would not, for example, test the poison on the fowl as though it were simply a natural poison, without putting any question to it at all, for this would be a foolish waste of poison. When an oracle contradicted itself, answering 'yes' and 'no' to exactly the same question, they would not doubt the value of oracles in general. They would merely argue that in this particular case there had been some fault in the procedure or the poison.

In the book already mentioned (p. 123) Polanyi has con-sidered the implications of this Zande system of belief for our understanding of the stability of belief and the 'fiduciary basis of knowledge' as he calls it, more generally. The Azande accept on traditional faith the assumption upon which their whole system of thought rests, and which, since it involves circular argument, defeats particular doubts:

So long as each doubt is defeated in its turn, its effect is to strengthen the fundamental convictions against which it was raised. 'Let the reader consider (writes Evans-Pritchard) any argument that would utterly demolish all Zande claims for the power of the oracles. If it were translated into Zande modes of thought it would serve to sup-port their entire structure of belief.' Thus the circularity of a con-ceptual system tends to reinforce itself by contact with every fresh topic.

The stability of belief, then, is shown by 'the way it denies to any rival conception the ground in which it might take root':

. . . a new conception, e.g. that of natural causation, which would take the place of Zande superstition, could be established only by a whole series of relevant instances, and such evidence cannot ac-cumulate in the minds of people if each of them is disregarded in its turn for lack of the concept that would lend significance to it.

Such is a philosopher's and scientist's account of what anthro-pologists have called 'collective representations', categories of thought which are absolutely assumed among members of a given society. In Polanyi's words, 'by holding the same set of presuppositions they mutually confirm each other's interpretation of experience.'

Anthropologists have commonly followed Frazer, Malinowski and others, in distinguishing 'magic' from 'religion' by reference to the attitude of the practitioner and the techniques employed. Magic in this view achieves its ends through formulae and acts which are held to be intrinsically effective in a quasi-deterministic way; it is thus, according to Frazer, an erroneous form of science. Religion on the other hand involves a sense of dependence upon higher powers, whose help is supplicated and anger propitiated, but who are not subject to man's absolute control.

At the time when native categories of priest, sorcerer, doctor, and witch were badly confused by Europeans, sometimes with resulting injustice as when priests were punished as sorcerers or 'witch-doctors' for example, there was something to be said for this effort to clarify our own terms. Also in many cultures the people themselves do commonly distinguish between mystical operations undertaken for private individual ends, often at the expense of other members of the society, and those which are openly performed for the benefit of all. Durkheim and his followers based their religious sociology on a universally acknowledged division of activities and objects into 'sacred' and 'profane' and demonstrated up to a point that 'the sacred' was closely connected with the social, while the profane or secular embraced matters of private individual interest. Durkheim and his colleagues thus rejected those many minimal definitions of religion which made belief in gods or spirits a necessary distinguishing feature. They turned instead to a study of the relations between these two domains, the sacred, set apart from common life and hedged round by taboos and special prohibitions and observances, and the profane. And these were not to be regarded as simply opposed to one another (as good to evil, for example) but as radically different in kind. They were as two different worlds, and to pass from the profane to the sacred man must, in effect, be born anew, as is represented in so many rites of initiation, purification, and consecration all over the world.

But attempts at working definitions and classification are only a beginning, and can sometimes direct attention from the central problems. Whether we call the particular notions and actions we study magical or religious or magico-religious (a compound word which itself indicates that such terms raise difficulties) our interest is in the nature of belief and knowledge, and of symbolic action and expression, in specific social contexts. Zande witchcraft notions, as we have seen, involve a systematic interpretation of human experience which, for Azande, is given a particular kind of order and coherence in their witchcraft philosophy. Behind that philosophy also, if not frequently invoked, is a conception of a Divinity, a First Cause, in which the order of the whole world is grounded.

Among many other peoples, beliefs in witchcraft are less in evidence and play a smaller explanatory role. It is then what we should call 'religious' beliefs (or among many today, political ideologies or the theories of natural science) that provide an ultimate framework for men's understanding of themselves and the world. The creeds of the Presbyterian and Anglican churches had once done so for Frazer, Darwin and their likes, before creeds seemed to exclude truth rather than symbolize it.

In discussing magical and religious beliefs and rites we are considering particular humans' apprehensions of underlying order in their world, ways of discovering and announcing that order, and means of adapting themselves to it. With this in mind, it is instructive to consider first, rather than traditional religions, certain relatively modern cults whose genesis is well-documented; for in ancient religions the accretions of centuries sometimes make it difficult to isolate boldly the fundamental principles of religious belief and action. We shall consider then two relatively new religions: the Ghost Dance religions which spread among many North American Indian tribes at the end of the last century; and the hundreds, and probably thousands, of separatist sects and native churches which, evolving their own forms of religious beliefs and rites, have broken away from Christian missionary churches in Africa.

The Ghost Dance religion is a general term referring to a number of separate religious revivals spreading among many different American Indian groups at various times in the course of the nineteenth century. They had in common the belief that by performing certain ritual dances and other ceremonies, and adhering to ethical and other prescriptions revealed in dreams to leaders who taught them to their followers, they would in Lucy Mair's phrase 'bring an ideal world into being'. The dances and other rituals would unite men with their ancestors—hence the general name 'Ghost Dance'—in a world and way of life which fulfilled many traditional Indian aspirations, though war and all quarrelsomeness, particularly among Indians, were forbidden.

Of the varieties of Ghost Dance (known in the vernacular by various names) I confine myself to one well-described complex studied by Alexander Lesser and described in *The Pawnee Ghost Dance Hand Game* (1933). The incorporation of an old Indian guessing and gambling game into the new rituals is of special interest in this religion.

By the end of the nineteenth century the Pawnee, whose ancestral territories lay between the Mississippi and the Rocky Mountains, where they had originally lived by horticulture and hunting, had become displaced and demoralized wards of the United States government. Their culture and traditional forms of enjoyment—hunting, dancing, gambling, and feasting—had suffered seriously through the civilizing efforts of missionaries and government officials. In 1892, says Lesser, 'after the best efforts of the Pawnee to adjust themselves to living alongside the white man, the tribe had come to a cultural impasse, with nothing to look forward to and nothing to live by'.

In the 1890's, various forms of the Ghost Dance, and the visions and rules connected with it, were spreading from a centre among the Californian Paiute to neighbouring Indians and then much more widely afield, In 1891 Frank White, a Pawnee Indian away from home, took part in the Ghost Dance among the Comanche and Wichita Indians of Oklahoma.

Under the influence of the dance and the drug peyote, White fell into a trance, and in a vision saw a village in which a figure described as the 'Messiah', and his people, were dancing and singing. He joined the dance, and learnt songs in his own Pawnee language. Later in the year he returned north to organize the dance and introduce connected rituals and doctrines among his own people. People were to prepare for the coming of the kingdom by dancing and other activities and abstentions, especially by abstaining from ploughing.

To turn away from certain practical activities and renounce certain material goods and advantages are features of millenarian movements in other parts of the world; but here also it is consistent with what seems to have been a deeply felt Indian revulsion against the white man's unrestrained exploitation of the earth. As one prophet (the Smohalla later mentioned (p. 134)) expressed it:

You ask me to plow the ground. Shall I take a knife and tear my mother's bosom? Then when I die she will not take me to her bosom to rest. You ask me to dig for stone. Shall I dig under her skin for her bones? Then when I die I cannot enter her body to be born again. . . .

It was of course basically the Americans' appetite for developing the continent which had resulted in the dispossession and degradation of the Indians. Frank White's religion was to create a different scale of values, and one in part recovered from an Indian past.

At first White taught the few songs he knew, some of them in Wichita and Arapaho, and organized the singers and the dancers in a simple form of liturgy. As more and more people joined his original group, the arrangements became more complex and formalized. White and his acolytes used a special sacred tipi where the dancers had their faces painted, and from where they came out to lead the dance. In dancing, the congregation fell into trances and made contact with another world:

From time to time those who fell would get up and tell what they had seen. Each had a message from the other world, and had learned songs. These visions became sanctions not only for special developments of the Ghost Dance and of the hand game, but also for important revivals of old aspects of Pawnee life, before this had ceased to function.

Those who acted and believed in this way (now as it were members of a church) were to be saved, and live on in an Indian Paradise when, as was predicted and imminently expected, a high wind would destroy the whites and the half-castes.

The ritual and ceremonial surrounding the Ghost Dance involved most importantly a preliminary pipe-smoking ceremony with special actors and elaborately formalized gestures, in which a blessing was given to the dancers. For the performance of all these ceremonies, the area of ground around White's tipi was divided up for the 'rituale' as a choreographer divides a stage, or as a church is divided, to give sacred meanings to special orientations. The cardinal points of the compass in particular had religious meanings attached to them. Connected with such religious meanings, there were also symbolic representations drawn partly from Indian and partly from Christian sources. Thus, one who was referred to as 'the Child of the Father in Heaven' is said to have appeared in a vision to teach the ritual and the doctrine of the smoke offering, parts of which were connected in meaning with a complex traditional star mythology. To this mythology Christ's crucifixion was assimilated since a cross was the Pawnee sign for 'star'.

With this eclectic integration of myths, beliefs, and rites, went an elaborate and coherent symbolism. Eagle or crow feathers were worn by some of the participants because the Pawnee thought of the eagle and the crow as high- and far-flying birds with penetrating vision and knowledge of distant matters. Their feathers were held to assist in producing the visionary states of the Ghost Dance. More particularly the crow was thought of as a bird which could find what it searched for, and would help people to find what they had lost—basically their old integrity. It is interesting to note that as Frank White's Ghost Dance religion developed, the eagle and crow, whose feathers had originally been used according to individual preference or knowledge, began to be seen in symbolic opposition, according to their different qualities, and were associated with opposing sides in the ritual Hand Game which formed an important adjunct to the Ghost Dance. Here is a simple example of the growth of a 'liturgy' and 'rituale', through the formalization of features which had first been accidental or haphazard, however imaginatively appropriate.

The traditional hand games of the North American Indians were originally guessing and gambling games, in which opposing teams, in pairs of individuals, guessed in which hand their opponents concealed a counter, though in forms of play of extreme elaboration and complication. Tallies were kept by the leaders, bets were placed on the results, and that team won which guessed most accurately. The games were basically competitions to show who had the greater 'luck', which the Indians thought of as positive quality—even quantity—of virtue, prestigious in itself and necessary for the successful conduct of life.

In the Hand Game played as an adjunct to the Ghost Dance religion, the gambling element was removed. Richer ceremonial and insignia were introduced, some of them drawn from old Pawnee symbolism of colours and natural objects. Tally sticks, for example, were made of the traditionally sacred cedar and dogwood, and were divided up into groups associated with different directions, basically the northern and southern horizons, which in turn were associated with different colours, the dark for the northern horizon, the bright for the southern horizon. There were altars with ordered arrangements of the sacred pipes and other *materia sacra*. The opponents or players took up their positions in formal relation to the altars. All this and much more elaboration of symbolic action developed around the fundamental interest of the Indians in solemnly discovering which had the greater 'luck'—or, to put it into terms which perhaps convey more of the real meaning in our own culture, which was more blessed.

This local Indian religion exhibits some common basic features of religion everywhere, even where the deep element of social protest and overwhelming nostalgia for the past— specific features of the Ghost Dance—are not significantly present: that is, myth, here represented by visions, coming from beyond present practical experience, which validates formal rituals and ceremonials: the doctrine of obligations and abstentions, here fairly simple, which this ritual and mythological complex carries with it; the quest for insight, and truth represented in many religions as 'illumination', and the creation in ritual and myth of a particular and coherent pattern of meanings, in terms of which the worshippers understand the order of the world and their relation to it. These go with differentiation of roles of the actors in the sacred play (here in the Ghost Dance Hand Game, the word 'play' is even literally appropriate) and the evaluation of spaces and objects in the material world according to the position they are assigned in this whole structure of thought and imagination and action. (Very widespread, in this evaluation, are sets of symbolic oppositions: good/evil, sky/earth, male/female, etc. The opposition of right and left, often equated respectively with the fortunate and the unfortunate, the male and the female, and the strong and the weak, has particularly interested social anthropologists since Robert Hertz's *La Prééminence de la main droite* (translated by Rodney and Claudia Needham in *Death and the Right Hand*, 1960).)

Two more, and shorter examples, further illustrate this characteristic activity of the religious imagination in symbolic and poetic thought. Those whom Sundkler in his *Bantu Prophets in South Africa* (1948) has called 'the Zionists' are independent native churches in South Africa, deriving ultimately from an American pentecostal church. They have developed different forms of syncretist religion with emphasis on healing, speaking with tongues, and purification by rites and the observation of taboos. Of one such church, Sundkler writes:

. . . Zionists regard their Zion Church as the court of heaven. The positions in the church house at T— of prophet X's Salem Church show clearly how the church is a replica of the heavenly temple: at the altar is sitting prophet X himself, 'the Judge' (*u Mahluli*) in episcopal vestments. . . . If he is absent . . . he has gone to the vestry where he is speaking to God through his 'Heavenly Telephone'. Near the altar are also the twelve prophets and the twelve apostles, the former in purple, the latter in white. In front of these are seated the Brides and Bridegrooms of the Lamb, some eighty to a hundred young men and girls, all in white. In the four corners of the nave of the church four men in white vestments stand silently: they are the four cardinal points, North, South, East, and West. The 'Hospital' is—logically—in the middle of the church: here are gathered the sick and those who are specially set aside to pray for them. . . .

and he adds: 'Their collective experience has provided a consistent "dream-geography" of heaven.'

Here then, again, a religion provides a distinctive patterning of experience, a map of the psyche and the world which, for believers, is held to represent the situation of man in true proportion and scale. This aspect of religions is well and succinctly illustrated in a detail from the religion of another American Indian prophet of the type earlier described, the prophet Smohalla.

In his great work *The Ghost Dance Religion and the Sioux Outbreak of 1890* (14th Report of the Bureau of Ethnology, 1892–3) James Mooney gives a description of the religion and doctrine of Smohalla, in which he reproduces a sketch of the heraldic flag which flew from his flagstaff. It is like this:

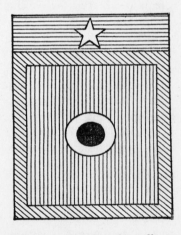

The field was yellow, representing the yellow grass of summer in that part of the world. The green border represented the boundaries of the world, green suggesting the moist greenery of mountains, and the band outside and above this was blue with a white star. The patch in the centre was red. Smohalla described his flag in the following terms:

This is my flag, and it represents the world. God told me to look after my people—all are my people. There are four ways in the world —north and south and east and west. I have been in all those ways. This is the centre. I live here. The red spot is my heart—everybody can see it. The yellow grass grows everywhere around this place. The green mountains are far away all round the world. There is only water beyond—salt water. The blue (referring to the blue cloth strip) is the sky, and the star is the north star. That star never changes; it is always in the same place. I keep my heart on that star. I never change.

In Melanesia, cults have arisen which have as part of their object to gain for their adherents European manufactured goods, known as 'cargo', which hitherto seem to have arrived only for Europeans. For this reason they are known as 'cargo cults' or 'cargo movements'. The political element in some of them has already been referred to (p. 67). K. O. L. Burridge, in *Mambu* (1960), describes how

participants . . . engage in a number of strange and exotic rites and ceremonies the purpose of which is, apparently, to gain possession of European manufactured goods. . . . Large decorated houses, or 'aeroplanes' or 'ships' made of wood, bark, and palm thatch bound together with vines, may be built to receive the goods, and participants may whirl, shake, chant, dance, foam at the mouth, or couple promiscuously in agitated attempts to obtain the cargo they want.

But something other than greed for material possessions is involved. Burridge says:

The most significant theme in cargo movements seems to be moral regeneration: the creation of a new man, the creation of new unities, the creation of a new society. . . . And both new man and new society are to be a true amalgam or synthesis, not a mixture of European and Kanaka forms and ideals.

These are religions largely created or initiated by charismatic leaders, as Max Weber called them, and bear the marks of consistency of a single dominating personality. But even then their coherence is not that of a logically thought out, rational scheme of ideas produced by one mind only. After the initial appeal of the leader's definition and interpretation of a particular social experience, others make their contributions to ritual and doctrine. The 'vision' of one man then becomes accepted by his followers as a source of their distinctive collective experience, of which their own visions are part. D. F. Pocock observes in *Social Anthropology* (1961):

These societies . . . were being subjected to a gathering flood of external experience which finally increased beyond the 'stretch' of the indigenous categories that might render it meaningful. . . . The social forms of communication appear inadequate. The society is as near to atomization as it could be. The last resort is a new stress upon the individual as that society conceives it, an emphasis upon history, upon individual possession by spirits, upon the individually inspired leader.

Messianic and millenarian cults arise in special historical circumstances, involving usually a strong sense of social deprivation in their adherents; but, eccentric in some details as these religions may be, we can see in them basic characteristics of other religions in which the historical factors affecting the growth of ritual and doctrine are more difficult to ascertain. In such religions, it is traditional teaching, more or less formalized according to the society, which establishes in the minds of believers a particular interpretation of cosmic order—a cosmogony, cosmology, and sometimes a cosmography—and a confidence in prescribed means of understanding and adapting to that order.

Religious conceptions and symbolism then unify the understanding of human experience, by emphasizing certain aspects of it (which differ from religion to religion) and placing them in a significant order and relationship one with another. Thus it is that the crises of human life—birth, initiation, marriage, death—are surrounded by rites and ceremonies in great variety, as Van Gennep observed in his great study of them, *Les Rites de passage* (1909, Eng. trans. 1960). By initiation ceremonies, for example, the young are made into adults, and their relations with the whole community then change. It is not unusual in these ceremonies for the initiate to undergo a symbolic death, so he may be born again as an adult. In ceremonies at death again, the relations between the dead and the living are defined and ordered. Secondary burial, when after a period the corpse is disinterred and reburied, among some peoples establishes the deceased as now finally one of the dead, whereas before he had not fully as we say 'passed over'. A Nuer man for whom the mortuary ceremonies had been performed during a long absence from home, when his death had been presumed, but who returned alive, was still regarded, so we are told, as a living ghost in the village.

Integration, whether of the self, the community, or the universe, is a characteristic, explicit religious concern. In an ancient Egyptian hymn to Ptah-tanu, quoted by Max Muller in his *Introduction to the Science of Religion* (1873), the god is made a figure of this integration: '. . . thou hast put together the earth, thou hast united thy limbs, thou hast reckoned thy members, what thou hast found apart, thou hast put in its place . . .' and in a passage from a contemporary life of the Emperor Akbar quoted by the same author, the King is represented as having a divinely conferred insight into order and unity behind the diversity of appearance:

. . . for a king possesses, independent of men, the ray of Divine wisdom, which banishes from his heart everything that is conflicting. A king will therefore sometimes observe the element of harmony in a multitude of things, or sometimes, reversely, a multitude of things in that which is apparently one.

In this picture of the enlightened ruler, idealized as it is, there is yet an element of sociological truth. The actual social role of leaders like the Grand Sanusi of Cyrenaica or 'divine kings' (like the King of the Shilluk earlier mentioned (Chap. 3, p. 66)) does in part derive from their religious status. By placing them theoretically above local oppositions among their people this status sometimes enables them to symbolize a deeper unity, putting them, more than others, in a position to reconcile those who are in conflict.

Numberless and immensely varied cosmogonic and cosmological myths also represent, with rich imagery, the establish-
ment and nature of the cosmic orders of different peoples, and
provide the full context of their religious practices. A common
theme in these myths is the creation of a physically and morally
ordered universe, out of chaos and darkness. The Maori of
New Zealand, according to Elsdon Best, speak of an original
state of 'night' before Sky and Earth appeared. This 'night', in
Maori, signifies not only simple night-time, but also the under-
world of the dead, and the period of human existence before
birth and after death. It implies the darkness of the unknown,
from which a sequence of forces and conditions developed
generating, eventually, the intelligible Maori universe into
being. Maori interest in genealogy leads them to explain the
developments of this earliest period by genealogical tables re-
cited, in varying versions, by a trained priestly class, and in
which personified forces appear as ancestors of a kind. One
such table has

. . . such names as Te Kune, Te Pupuke, Te Hihiri, Te Mahara, Te
Hinengaro, and Te Manako, ere coming to the primal parents Sky
and Earth. These expressions may be rendered as 'the conceiving',
'the flowing forth' (or swelling), 'the persevering' (or thinking),
'the thought' (or power of thinking), and 'the longing' or desiring.

Next in this Maori Genesis come Sky and Earth, then close together. From their mating many gods of the Maori pantheon
were born:

. . . When these children were born, the Earth Mother was shrouded
in darkness, the only sign of light was the feeble glimmer of a glow-
worm. . . . Sky and Earth were in close contact, for the Sky parent
was closely embracing the Earth Mother. . . .

The god Tane, one of the children of this mating and the pro-
genitor of mankind, then proposed to his brothers that the
parents should be separated, 'that the Sky should be forced up-
ward that they might enjoy freedom of movement and the air
of space'. His brother Whiro (the god personifying evil, darkness, and death) objected, and when Tane succeeded in separa-

ting Sky and Earth, remained within the Earth. Tane brought
light and life to men, and symbolizes light, life, and fertility.

In this much abbreviated version of the complex Maori
mythologies dealing with the creation, are features very similar
to some in creation myths told by peoples with whom the Maori
could have had no historical contact. An original chaos, dark
and undifferentiated, gives way to a particular ordered world
with a space for human beings to live in and the light by which
they can see and know. Among many peoples, it is some human
act which creates an initial separation of Sky and Earth. This
is often figured also as a separation of God and Man, and is
therefore logically the origin of religious practice, in representing the differentiation and separation of the divine and the
human. Very widespread are myths which explain the division
of Sky and Earth, and God and Man, by the act of a woman.
According to the Dinka of the Sudan the first woman, trying
to pound more grain than God had allowed for human requirements, struck God and the Sky with a long-handled pestle.
Offended, God withdrew from the earth, and men have since
had to propitiate him, especially in sickness and death, both
originally unknown.

The idea that the creation of the world was a giving of reality
to mere appearance or potential, the emergence of the actual,
palpable world from a dream or thought, is found in myth. It
appears very clearly in the following, from the Uitota Indians of
South America—one example of the poetic metaphysic with
which the social anthropologist (and the depth psychologist,
from whom in this field we may have much to learn) is often
presented:

In the beginning there was nothing but mere appearance. Nothing
really existed. It was a phantasm, an illusion, that our father touched;
something mysterious it was that he grasped. Nothing existed.
Through the agency of a dream our father, He-who-is-appearance-
only Nainema, pressed the phantasm to his breast and then was sunk
in thought. Not even a tree existed that might have supported this
phantasm, and only through his breath did Nainema hold this illusion attached to the thread of a dream. He tried to discover what was
at the bottom of it, but he found nothing. 'I have attached that

which was non-existent', he said. There was nothing. Then our
father tried again and investigated the bottom of this something and
his fingers sought the empty phantasm.

He tied the emptiness to the dream thread, and pressed the magical
glue substance on it. Thus by means of his dream did he hold it like
the fluff of raw cotton.

He seized the bottom of the phantasm and stamped upon it re-
peatedly, allowing himself finally to rest upon the earth of which he
had dreamt.

The earth phantasm was now his. Then he spat out saliva re-
peatedly so that forests might arise. He lay upon the earth and set the
covering of heavens above it. He drew from the earth the blue and
white heavens and placed them above.

Here, and also in Maori belief, appears a theme to which early
writers on 'primitive religion' often did little justice: the very
high value set on the power of thought, on knowledge, intelligence, and insight. In *La Pensée sauvage* (1962) Professor Lévi-
Strauss has convincingly illustrated the practical, even systematic, knowledge which many peoples once thought to lack intellectual curiosity actually seek, and obtain, by exploring their
environment.

Knowledge and intelligence are all the more conditions of
survival and success where the material advantages of our own
kind of civilization are lacking. It is knowledge and intelligence,
often represented also in trickery, cunning, and deceit, which
characterize what are called the 'culture heroes' who are held
to have contributed much to the spiritual and cultural heritage
of the societies to which they belong.

But when Jacob deceives his father and tricks Esau, or when
some other heroic trickster (sometimes a man or demiurge,
sometimes figured in folklore as an animal—the hare, the spider,
the coyote are well-known examples) outwits his enemies and
even his friends, we should be wrong to conclude that the
peoples who admire these acts do not also in their ordinary
lives set some store by truthfulness and uprightness. These
heroic deceptions are remembered as showing the power and
value of cleverness and knowledge, often associated with luck
or blessing also. Ethical judgements are here irrelevant or are

suspended. Hence 'holy' men, even in religions which contain a strong ethical teaching, are not always personally exemplars of the conventional morality of their societies.

People now brought up in the traditions of the universal religions are accustomed indeed to a more direct integration of ethical and religious prescription. St Augustine pointed to this in arguing the superiority of Christianity to paganism: the pagan gods, for him when converted from them, were inferior in that they gave no moral teaching and were themselves represented as committing shameful acts. But in many pagan societies, as often in practice in our own, it is the parents and the elders who primarily inculcate morality. The gods, or some of the gods, are simply its ultimate sanction. In themselves, they are beyond human moralizing.

It will have been apparent that religious and magical 'beliefs', as we call them, are often for those who hold them rather a kind of knowledge and theory of the nature of the universe and of man. From this point of view, there is some point of comparison between such beliefs and the theories of natural science. Robin Horton has even suggested that a modern physicist might become aware of 'a logical resemblance between the gods of primitive peoples and the ultimate particles and other theoretical entities of his own science'.

The differences of course are very marked, and most particularly in the quest for certain kinds of universal truths which characterizes the procedure of natural science. Magical and religious beliefs or theories may indeed be attested *in* experience, either of the individual or the community of believers; but they are not systematically and coldly tested *against* experience over as wide a range of instances as possible. Hence the many occasions when magical or religious expectations are not satisfied in practice are not set against the few when they are. There is a well-known passage in Livingstone's *Missionary Travels* in which a conversation (perhaps not entirely *ipsissima verba*) between Livingstone and an African Rain-Doctor or Rain-Maker underlines this difference. Livingstone accuses the Rain-Doctor of waiting for the clouds, then using his medicines and taking the credit for having brought the rain. The Rain-Doctor replies:

... we are both doctors and not deceivers. You give a patient medicine. Sometimes God is pleased to heal him by means of your medicine. Sometimes not—he dies. When he is cured, you take the credit for what God does. I do the same. Sometimes God grants us rain, sometimes not. When he does, we take the credit of the charm. When a patient dies you don't give up trust in your medicine. Neither do I when no rain falls. ...

The medical doctor answers:

I give medicine to living creatures within my reach, and can see the effect though no cure follows. ... God alone can command the clouds. Only try and wait patiently. God will give us rain without your medicines.

To which the Rain-Doctor says:

Well, I always thought white people were wise until this morning. Whoever thought of making a trial of starvation? Is death pleasant then?

Ironically the Rain-Doctor's beliefs had something more in common with those of modern scientific rain-makers than had those of Livingstone. The Rain-Doctor thought to make rain by the use of medicines and techniques, and it is by 'medicines' and techniques that clouds are seeded today, whatever also may be thought to be the efficacy of prayer.

As religious and magical beliefs involve definitions of physical, intellectual, and moral order, part of religious practice consists in the attempt to discover the relations between that order and particular events and situations of human life. Religious and magical practices are thus often concerned with the searching out of truths which, it is thought, men must know for their own good, and which go beyond common knowledge or purely rational deduction. Zande witch-doctors and oracles, the visions of the Ghost Dance and ecstasies of the Bantu prophets' congregations, the supposedly superior wisdom and insight of divine kings—all these are examples of this urgent interest in truths which are thought to lie beyond practical or purely rational investigation.

Among the Polynesians the spiritual power or *mana* (a word which, like *taboo* from the same part of the world, has become an anthropological term) of a priest was demonstrated in the truth of his predictions, and from all over the world there are examples of the value set upon a superior grasp of 'truth', whether of past, present, or future—in the visionary medicine men or *shamans* of the Eskimo, in African priests and diviners, in the mystics and saints and prophets of the universal religions, and even in the petty clairvoyants of our own rationalistic civilization. These are more discredited in theory, perhaps, than in practice, as the business of horoscopes, prediction and so on shows. A Maori diviner, seeking the cause of sickness, expresses this constituent of religious and magical practice in his spell or prayer:

> A seeking a searching
> To seek whither?
> To search the land, to seek the origin,
> To seek out the base, to search the unknown
> To seek out the *atua* [spirit]
> May it be effectual.

Another aspect of it is implied in the solemn custom of calling the gods to reveal, or witness or guarantee truth in trials by ordeal, swearing of oaths, and the consultation of oracles.

Sacrifice is the central act of many religions: and on this subject Dr Sundkler quotes a revealing statement by one of the foremost founders of independent African churches, a Zulu named Isaiah Shembe. 'Isaiah Shembe,' he says, 'though reticent in speaking to Europeans on the subject of sacrifices, nevertheless insisted on the need of them: "They hold people together by blood. The Gate of Heaven is opened through sacrifices." '

There are overtones of Christian teaching here, especially in the reference to Heaven. But the suggestion that sacrifice in some sense 'holds people together' does not derive exclusively from Christianity, still less from the peculiarities of belief of this African sect. Looking at sacrifice in the simple, factual, even naturalistic way in which an anthropologist must begin his study, it is possible to see considerable sociological truth in Shembe's view, quite apart from any theological or mystical meaning it may also have.

Many different kinds of sacrifice have been distinguished—sacrifice as a gift to the gods; as a sign of communion with them and a way of gaining strength from them; sacrifice as atonement, as self-abnegation, as immolation or destruction for the divinity, and so forth. But sacrifice in general involves the notion of an offering; and among the commonest types of sacrificial offerings are those made by so many peoples of the world for the dead ancestors of their own families.

Such offerings are found not only among so-called primitive peoples but also in the literate civilizations of Eastern and Western antiquity. They vary much in kind, from expressions of filial regard—small gifts of food or drink or other symbolic acts of commemoration—to blood sacrifice itself. The motives behind the services rendered to ancestors, ghosts, or family gods, are similarly varied.

Yet there is a common element in what is often rather misleadingly called 'ancestor worship'. Whatever the nature of the offering, or the reason behind it, it does perpetuate the memory of the dead; and it does acknowledge that the living and the dead belong to a single community, wider than that of the living alone. And this is not simply a pious belief. There obviously is continuity, biological and cultural, between the living and the dead. We are partly formed by the past, even the distant past. Sacrificial offerings for ancestors symbolically recognize this. Further, those who remember their dead together, and share the same dead, also of necessity emphasize their living relationships among themselves: commemoration of the ancestor is affirmation of the range of relationships he created among the living, a holding together of all those who count him important in their past.

So in the many societies, both historical and of the present, where family, kin, and lineage are of more importance than in our kind of state, common sacrifice is a sign of common interests, and an act which asserts and promotes them. It represents a common life, and not only on an ideal or metaphorical plane, but in the day-to-day practical affairs of human co-operation. Sometimes this may be observed in detail in the very way in which the flesh of a sacrificial animal is shared. Among some Nilotic peoples of the Sudan, oxen are the preferred victims: the ox is brought out and tethered to a peg in the centre of the people; they pray and invoke the gods over it; the priest, in some cases, leads the prayers which are repeated by the congregation. Sicknesses and misfortunes are put 'upon the back' of the victim. In its death it will carry them away—another Christian theme which is not exclusively Christian. Finally, the beast is killed and its flesh is divided according to strict rule among different groups within the family and the community. The officiating priest has his allotted portions, as do the mother's and the father's kin of those making the sacrifice, the old people of the community, and so on. The whole beast therefore actually figures in its body the social relationships of those present at its death. The integrity of the local society is incarnate, as it were, in the victim.

A similar theme of holding people together, and the recognition of a common life in religious acts—though not strictly in sacrifice—may be found in some forms of totemism. Among many peoples, the relationship existing between whole groups of people, notably those claiming common descent and belonging to the same clan, is symbolized by a totem. Totems are of many kinds, but are often one or another species of animal, sometimes regarded as an ancestor of the clan. A common totem therefore stands for a community of interests of one sort or another as McLennan (p. 15) recognized. Among the Australian aborigines, let us say, a clan which has as its totem the kangaroo will pay special attention to kangaroos, and perform ceremonies from time to time to increase their numbers.

Members of that clan are thus related in the kangaroo, and identified as a group with common interests by reference to the animal. On ceremonial occasions, pieces of the flesh of the totemic animal may be solemnly eaten, often by old men or guardians of the group. Earlier writers—Robertson Smith and Durkheim among them—saw in this eating of the flesh of a totem,

which was also in some sense sacred, one of the elemental features of all sacrifice: communion with the god and between the
worshippers in the eating of its flesh. This interpretation would
not fit what we now know of the varied forms of totemism;
certainly there are peoples who do not interpret the eating of
the flesh of the victim after sacrifice as a religious communion.
Yet again the sharing of a sacrificial beast, or of the flesh of a
totemic animal, is in fact a sign and reaffirmation of relationship and community of interest.

What are these common interests? In those societies where
the state does not offer its protection an individual depends first
on his kinsmen. To be without kin, by chance or war or other
misfortune, is to be in danger, to be helpless. So an isolated individual must find a group which will accept him—first perhaps
as a friend, or servant; then in some sense as a kinsman. And
either he, or his descendants, are finally guaranteed full protection when they are admitted, according to their place, to a full
share in the sacrificial rites. Members of a well-defined political
community sacrifice together; and those who sacrifice together
have their share of protection by that community. So a sacrifice
may often involve expressions of hostility to enemies—even displays against death itself. People sacrifice not only positively
for themselves, but negatively against those forces that would
destroy them.

The service of family ancestors and family gods, or even of
clan ancestors and clan gods, is the duty of groups of kinsmen:
others are ultimately excluded from such family cults. Along
with these cults in many societies there are others, which em-
brace wider communities, not only of kin but also of neighbours and fellow tribesmen or townsmen. Those who live in
the same territory, who share a land and co-operate in its protection and prosperity, then have gods to which sacrifice and
other services may be rendered on behalf of the whole population of a town or region.

There is little or no evidence for supposing that the worship
of the gods of such larger communities is everywhere a later
historical development than cults of ancestors and family gods.
Both kinds of cult often exist side by side, as do their adherents;

together they reflect the total complex order of the communities which are drawn together in them. Also many—perhaps all—'polytheistic' peoples seem to exhibit at times a monotheistic train of thought. The various gods and spirits presiding over the fortunes and interests of different sections of the society and different aspects of the physical world may on occasion be seen as manifestations, not, it is true, of one supreme personal God, but at least of a single divine principle informing all the gods. For the ancient Greeks too, it would appear, Zeus, though a distinct divine figure, could also stand for the gods, divinity in the abstract.

Gods of various kinds seem to merge in this single notion of 'the divine' when peoples have in mind the human community as a whole in relation to higher powers. Sacrifice, even to commemorate particular family ancestors or the guardian spirits of a clan or a place, is often accompanied by service to a divinity of all men. In Dinka sacrifices I have seen, two separate victims may be offered, one to the totemic spirits of the clan providing the sacrifice, and one to a god in the sky who watches over all the human creation. It is as though the act of sacrifice itself, turning men's attention to a kind of being different from and superior to their own, also suggests, besides local ties and loyalties, a widening circle of common human concerns.

But the bonds that might hold together a potentially universal society can scarcely be suggested, felt, and known, except in the experience which unites much smaller groups of people—the family, the clan, the village or town or guild. So it is that these particular experiences of communal living are symbolized in local deities; and sacrifice, the central feature of service of the gods, focuses attention upon the common values of the worshippers in focusing attention on the gods. From an anthropological view it is finally irrelevant whether or not these gods exist outside living human consciousness of them. Nor do we need to inquire into the deeper personal, spiritual, and psychological grounds of sacrifice. The sociological meaning of sacrifice has begun to be suggested when we have accepted it as a way of serving the gods, and seen what those gods mean in relation to social life and human relations, how they correspond to the sharing of interests within different communities and sections of communities. From this point of view sacrifice to a common god is a sign and a strengthening of the common life. From other points of view it has other meanings.

If the sociological point of view, as far as it goes, has some truth in it, we see why it is that so widely throughout the world the situation of sacrifice is thought to demand peace and agreement between those who sacrifice together. In the ordinary course of social life, even members of a single and affectionate family may be at odds with each other; but in a religious ceremony it is often explicitly required that these differences should at least appear to be overcome. So, to give one of many examples, it is said that the duties of a high priest among the Gã peoples of Ghana are:

... not only to officiate at public worship, and give the god its daily or weekly libations, but to interpret to the people the wishes of the god ... The peace of the town is one of his first concerns ... He does not like his children to quarrel. ... [1]

And if public worship, of which sacrifice in one form or another is often the typical act, springs from a community of interests, so it demands, and probably to some extent creates, a group at peace within itself.

Sacrifice therefore often plays an important part in ceremonies for confirming a peace. In an account of a peace-making ceremony among the Shilluk, this is represented in an unusual image. After the victim had been speared and fallen, we are told:

The two factions moved close together. The animal was then cut open, and some of the contents of the stomach were taken by the old men, and thrown on the young men. The thought was that the animal eats a bit here and a bit there, but in the stomach it all becomes one mass. Even so the individuals of the two factions were to become one.

Here it seems that collective sacrifice expresses and confirms the intentions of those who offer it to regard themselves as

[1] M. J. Field, *Religion and Medicine of the Gã People*, 1937.

members of a single peaceful community. The concerns of any one become the concerns of all; as is seen very clearly in the general primitive belief in the efficacy of public sacrifice for curing those individuals who are sick and helping those who are barren. Why it should be that beliefs in the sacrificial death of a victim as a means to life and harmony for the people are so widely held raises other and different questions. There may be other means of producing the same effects; but that sacrifice does, as Shembe said, 'hold people together' would seem to be a belief founded on practical experience among many people of the world. It has been upon this ground of experience that so many different theological inquiries and reflections have been based.

7

How Anthropologists Think

... and thus by placing the same thing in various relationships, we are able to deduce new relationships and new truths.

Karl Marx

How Natives Think, the title chosen for the English translation of Lucien Lévy-Bruhl's serious work *Les Fonctions mentales dans les sociétés inférieures* (1912), suggests nothing of his deep, self-questioning concern with the nature of thought generally. At the end of that study, he makes it clear that it was his own kind of thought, and that of his intellectual contemporaries, which he sought to understand better through the examination of ethnographic literature on very different peoples:

On the one hand, the claims of reason desire to impose themselves on all that is imagined and thought. On the other hand, the collective representations of the social group, even when clearly prelogical and mystic by nature, tend to subsist indefinitely, like the religious and political institutions of which they are the expressions and in another sense the bases.

So, he says, even when we try to reach objectivity in sociological study, our reasoning is with difficulty liberated from the conventional assumptions of our own age and society:

Hence arise mental conflicts as acute, and sometimes as tragic, as conflicts between rival duties. They too proceed from a struggle between collective habits, some time-worn and others more recent, differently orientated. . . . Undoubtedly it is thus that we should account for the so-called struggle of reason with itself, and for that which is real in its antinomies.

Lévy-Bruhl was considering a different climate of thought from that of today: but when we study man in society, we are still, as it were, both subject and object of inquiry, and it is within the logic of social anthropology itself that we should finally examine some of the ideas we use and have used to represent the ideas of others.

In earlier chapters there are examples of observations distorted, and theory misdirected, by prejudices, assumptions, and ideals belonging to their own particular times and places in European intellectual history, and no more than that. Social anthropologists today are free, it is safe to say, from such conspicuous bias, but as they would be the first to admit, when human beings write about human beings it is not easy to eliminate all personal and social idiosyncrasy. Almost all monographs on other peoples can be made to yield a good deal of information about their authors also, and we cannot pretend that more generally social ideas of the time in which modern anthropology has developed have not affected its findings.

Since the first world war at least, there has been for example a strong current of a kind of liberalism in anthropological thought, which may sometimes have idealized the integration, stability, and equilibrium of many societies before European contact. Understandable as this is as a humane reaction against gross misrepresentations of 'primitive' life, it still has little to do with social anthropology now as a scientific discipline. It assumes (like the writers of the *Année Sociologique*) a moral purpose and virtue in 'society' itself, realized to a greater or lesser degree in any particular society according to the sociologist's assessment. Even with great care it is difficult, when considering the social function of customs or institutions, to avoid such teleology, and in works on 'social change' particularly, all oppositions, inconsistencies, and violence in the supposedly traditional social order have sometimes been represented as working ultimately towards its conservation. The reality and consequences of radical conflict have tended to be played down, as anthropologists have turned moralists.

And it is indeed hard for them, moral and social beings, to school themselves even in a professional capacity to detachment from the human affairs they study, intellectually desirable as that must be. When Margaret Mead, who on her first visit to the Manus of New Guinea found them 'gay' as children but 'unlovable and unloving adults', on visiting them again after the last world war describes them as 'infused by their upbringing with an aspiration congruent with the more universal and humane forms of Western democracy', there appears the blending of human with scientific concerns which it is difficult entirely to avoid in this subject. As has been seen earlier, social anthropology owes much to a basically moral impetus, for the public that anthropologists could expect until the last ten years was inevitably more ethnocentric than that of today, with our vastly increased communications. It was not easy then to divide the practical and moral problems of human, and for the most part colonial, relations, from the problems of strictly sociological analysis. With the decline of colonial power and responsibility, such moral problems become less and less significant, and the kind of human understanding they sought seems no longer to advance us much in the theoretical study of society. Autonomous peoples do not require our 'sympathy'.

If moral involvement sometimes has been an obstacle to strictly sociological theory, another, related to it, has been the uncritical use of the word 'culture'. That anthropology is the study—and tends towards the appraisal—of cultures, an idea once particularly prevalent in Britain, and in America and Germany, dies hard. Certainly, social anthropologists still seek as rounded a knowledge as possible of the material and spiritual characteristics of the peoples they study, for it is impossible to know what kind of detail may eventually become theoretically significant, either for themselves or for others working in cognate fields. But unselective listing of cultural details—'culture traits'—has also inhibited the formation of the intellectual constructs which alone can express their interrelationships and hence the meaning of any one of them. As Marcel Proust (himself so immersed in detail) said of artistic representations, so of anthropological exposition:

One can place indefinitely in succession, in a description, the objects which figured in the place described: truth will not begin [to appear] until the moment when the writer will take two different objects, will place them in a relationship, analogue in the world of art to the unique relationship of the causal law in the world of science.

Even Malinowski's great book *Argonauts of the Western Pacific* is thick with cultural information that does not further the analysis, and may sometimes have retarded it, and it is a mark of his genius as an observer, as of his occasional lack of refinement as a thinker, that others have been able to interpret some of Malinowski's material more convincingly than he did himself.

Boas, Malinowski, and their students indeed made a basic point of trying to relate cultural facts in the way Proust desiderates, as when Malinowski describes the connection between kinship, magic, chieftainship, and technology in the culutral complex of Trobriand canoe-making. But despite the advances that this emphasis on social function made possible, much of the work it produced still remains basically descriptive. It relates in theory only what is conspicuously and inevitably co-present in reality, often making little explicit analytic contribution to the interpretation of social situations outside the original field of study.

A further source of confusion is when, as often, 'cultures' are treated as though they had a kind of unitary, organic life of their own, over and above the men and women in whose ideas and activities any culture is observed. Here the use of the word 'culture' has often diverted attention from realities of social relationship. Much has been written about what is called 'culture contact' in England, and 'acculturation' in America, but as E. R. Leach observed in *Political Systems of Highland Burma* (1954) it often does not take us far in understanding what actually happens when peoples of different 'culture' live side by side. This is partly because that word, as it is frequently used, has an impossibly wide range of reference. An example occurs

in a book of essays, *Continuity and Change in African Cultures* (ed.
W. R. Bascom and M. J. Herskovits, 1958), according to which

Culture includes not only social institutions and their derivative
forms of learned behaviour but also those manifestations of creativ-
ity whereby the artist produces something new and individual within
the range of forms and patterns which are part of his tradition . . . .
The study of culture involves not only the institutions that frame
man's reactions to fellow members of his society, but also the extra-
institutional aspects of human behaviour, including language, the
relation between language and behaviour, between personality and
culture, and the system of values that gives meaning to the accepted
forms of behaviour of a people.

But how is such a definition to be used in practice? In the same
book, we read:

Nigeria affords a classic example of the effects of cultural backgrounds on the course of recent events. The policy of indirect rule
was first applied among the Hausa in the north, where political
authority was centered in the Emir and where taxation, courts and
other governmental institutions comparable to those of Europe were
already in existence. It was extended with little difficulty to the
Yoruba, in the southwest, since their traditional political structure
was sufficiently similar.

Here the authors have been compelled, in a single paragraph,
to shift from 'cultural background' to 'social structure', for of
course by any definition of the term Yoruba and Hausa *culture*
are also very different, and could not explain their similar reactions to foreign rule.

It is not then cultures that meet, but human beings, with
different upbringing, possessions, interests, and expectations.
Misleading therefore are such expressions as 'the clash of cultures' or 'cultural barriers' when they disguise what are really
strong divergences of political, economic, moral, and aesthetic
views between different communities or sections of a community. Also too much has probably been heard, in anthropology, of the individual and social strains of assimilating two 'cultures', the problems of 'men of two worlds', and too little of
the long histories of cultural assimilation and integration.

For clarity of thought, then, it is necessary to distinguish between culture, as the sum total of material and moral resources of any population, and social systems. Peoples culturally heterogeneous are commonly drawn together in a single political system, and not only in modern states. On the other hand, cultural homogeneity is by no means always accompanied by political unity. The million or so Dinka of the Southern Sudan, and their neighbours the Nuer, are culturally very similar indeed; but politically they are divided into many mutually exclusive and often hostile tribes. To understand the relations between these, and their internal affairs, we have to investigate not the whole cultural reality, but an abstraction from it, 'social structure'.

The concept of social structure has undoubtedly been one of the main sources of theoretical advance in social anthropology, but it has not always been used (and it is not easy to use it) with any single consistent and precise meaning. Radcliffe-Brown, who reflected much on the matter, seems to have conceived of it as the whole complex of relations subsisting between members of any population, each individual being as it were a cell related in numerous ways to the rest. But it is difficult if not impossible to form any precise mental image of such a complex of relations; and others have thought of social structure as what Radcliffe-Brown himself called 'structural form', that is the form of institutionalized relations and group relations within any society, which differs from one to another. In either case, to study social structure is to posit that a society can be represented formally as sets of relations between isolable elements, or parts, of which it is constituted.

In practice social anthropologists have broken down this general concept—one difficult to handle for particular investigations, since it directs attention to too much at once—into others, like kinship structure, economic structure, and political structure, with narrower, more manageable fields of reference. In practice too, in modern times they have usually defined their societies (the largest units of their study) by political criteria, taking not the inhabitants of any 'culture area' or arbitrarily chosen geographical location as the primary object of study, but states or tribes. They have tried, on the whole, to represent first the political structure of these, before examining other structures of relationship—family and kinship, economic, religious and so forth.

In this we have to *start* with observations of cultural phenomena, and of how people behave and what they say about themselves, for social structure is not, of course, there to be seen. It is a latent pattern in social relations, discovered by analysing a large body of information, and providing an understanding of social events which transcends the complexity and confusion of concrete reality. How an anthropologist tries to arrive at this abstract formulation is best exhibited by considering actual examples, some of which have already been touched upon.

A good anthropological monograph looks as though it might have been produced without great difficulty, for it has already reduced to order the complications and problems presented by the mass of material collected piecemeal in day-to-day inquiries. Once the lineage principle in political structure (pp. 57–59) has been elucidated, for example, it seems obviously possible as a basis for political relations. People who are politically organized on this principle, it will be remembered, unite with those nearer to them in their genealogical tree, at every point, against those who are more remote. The elements in this political structure then are lineages (themselves conceptual), and the nature of the relationship between them is simply expressed as 'fission and fusion'. That does not seem as though it should have been hard to discover.

But the members of any lineage may be individually widely dispersed, and in any case they usually bear no external mark of their lineage membership. A lineage system is not apparent to the eye. It is a theory of political behaviour, according to which lineage members act by a kind of rule-of-thumb knowledge, which the social anthropologist expresses in more comprehensive and abstract terms. He thus represents the principles behind the political behaviour of the people he has studied, and in doing so hopes to provide a model to which political behaviour in other societies may be referred. This is not achieved

without systematic study and considerable comparative knowledge, and in fact the nature and importance of lineage segmentation were for long obscure to knowledgeable students of
politics, whose only model of political structure was that of the
state, with formal organs of government. What did not correspond to this model was not recognized as any form of political
order, and seemed anarchy. We now see that other models are
possible which enable us better to account for the facts, and it
has been by providing those that social anthropologists have progressively freed themselves from some of the limitations to our
understanding other systems of thought and action imposed by
the particular societies in which the subject first developed.
They have tried to think with their own minds, and with the
minds of others different from them.

How does an anthropologist thus translate what he has observed in, say, Nuer society, into the statement that their political structure is of the lineage-segmentary kind? It has been
usual in recent years for the student of any society to spend
some two years living there at close quarters with the people,
speaking their language and trying to share their interests.
What he sees and hears of in that period is not 'segmentary
lineage structure', but large numbers of people, many social
occasions, and much conversation. In time, some regularities
in behaviour can be discerned. Certain people are present at
weddings or sacrifices, others are absent: people divide themselves up for different purposes in different ways. And while all
this is being observed, the student is learning the language, and
thus becoming familiar with the social categories of the people
themselves.

So, in the case of the Nuer, it is found that a word, *cieng*, may
be translated as 'home' in a variety of contexts. It may refer,
according to where the speaker is, to the whole of Nuerland, or
to the territory of a tribe, or division of a tribe, or to a village,
or to a homestead. This relativity is paralleled by that of another
Nuer term, *thok dwiel*, literally meaning 'the mouth (doorway)
of the hut'. This term, it becomes clear, does not, like *cieng*,
refer to place, but to agnatic descent. A man's *thok dwiel* is his
descent group, and he is a member of as many groups, each

included in the next largest, as he counts significant ancestors in the male line. To these groups, the word 'lineage' is applied, and it is found that there are several lineages in each village. Lineages of common descent together form a clan, and one clan in each tribe, it is discovered, is accorded a different status from others as *diel*, which may be translated as 'aristocrats'. After further investigations, it appears that this aristocratic clan is distributed in lineages throughout the territorial sections of the tribe down to the village, and in each of these aristocrat lineages are the nuclei around which lineages of different descent are clustered. In the political relations of villages and tribal sections, these other lineages identify themselves with their local lineage of the aristocratic clan, and the genealogy of that clan thus provides a key to their alliances and hostilities. So it is now known that territorial segments associated with lineages are the elements or parts, in systematic relationship, in this form of political structure, and that their relationship is on a genealogical model. Further, in each tribe are found lineages of priests who do not belong to the politically central aristocratic clan, and can offer their services in peacemaking between political segments precisely because (like the Sanusiya Order in Cyrenaica described in pp. 63–65) they are not completely identified with any one of them. They are catalysts in the political relations of others. This, very summarily presented and simplified, is the way in which an anthropologist has identified a type of political structure and enabled us to understand ultimately in a few words how the political activity of hundreds of thousands of people, which has finally yielded that abstraction, is ordered.

When these findings from one people are presented, they advance our understanding of political principles among many others. Variants of this segmentary lineage structure, some slight, some greater, permit comparisons extending our understanding of political structures generally, and which would never have been possible from a less abstract formulation. Among the Alur of Uganda and the Congo for example, Aidan Southall found a combination of a kind of lineage segmentation with an element of rule, or at least personal leadership, by

houses of originally foreign Nilotic aristocrats among an indigenous, ethnically mixed population.

Among the Alur, the Nuer model does not as a whole apply
exactly, for the absence of any ruler is essential to it. Southall
therefore had to find another, that of what he called 'the segmentary state', in which lineage relations are combined with
those between chiefs and chiefs, and chiefs and commoners,
and the aristocrats themselves are the peacemakers. According
then to *Alur Society* (1953), the structural oppositions of lineage
segmentation are there greatly modified by 'structural comple-
mentarity' between two ethnic groups, the one, originally politically organized on a small scale only, receiving chiefs and
rainmakers from the other which, while also genealogically
segmented, provides the basis of a larger-scale polity. As
Southall illustrates, something similar is to be found among
peoples far from the Alur, and it teaches us something therefore
about elementary forms of the state. Alur states can be distinguished also from other forms of political structure which include rulers—for example from 'the conquest state', where a
conquering people has established control by force, and the relationship between rulers and ruled (here important elements
of political structure) is one of superordination and subordin-
ation, with a fixed assumption of social inequality, in complete
contrast with the ideally egalitarian principles of the lineage-
segmentary type of political structure.

Here are historical changes not known amongst peoples like
the Nuer from whose politics the classical account of segmentary lineage structure was derived; and as E. R. Leach in particular urged in *Political Systems of Highland Burma* earlier mentioned, change and diversity in the political elements of a society or of two societies of ideally different types which are yet in
practice assimilated to one another, raise interesting problems
for structural analysis. The recorded history of many of the
societies social anthropologists have studied is very exiguous,
and representations of their social structure have perforce been
derived from a knowledge of their condition during a relatively
short period of time, often producing an impression of a static
society. *The Sanusi of Cyrenaica*, where structural continuity and

change over a century or so are described, is a rare exception.

In some cases, there is indeed little reason to suppose that the anthropological model of the political structure of a society as it was during relatively few years would not have been equally correct for other periods of their history, for there is nothing to suggest that structural changes have occurred, and much to suggest that they have not.

This is so of the Nuer themselves, and the analysis of their traditional lineage segmentation was found to have an explanatory value for political alignments in the different setting of a Nuer local government council twenty or more years after it was first described. And structural principles inherent in other traditional systems have certainly persisted into changed social and cultural circumstances. A small example appears in a symposium *Social Change in Modern Africa* (ed. A. Southall, 1961) in a comment on the employment of servants by members of different African societies when they are working in towns. The Tutsi of Rwanda, it is said, who have in the past always exercised domination in their own society where a 'premise of inequality' has existed, aim at acquiring a servant before buying bicycles or radios like many others. In Kampala, the Ganda take non-Ganda servants, or unrelated Ganda, for it would be embarrassing and shameful to the whole family to take relatives as servants. For them, a servant is a servant. Not so among the Luo, 'with an egalitarian traditional system and very strong agnatic ties which transcend modern status differences', who are served by relatives, not openly in the capacity of servants, but as members of the household as in the traditional system where no master-servant relationship is found.

But where there is strong reason to infer that there has been radical historical change, or where evidence for it exists, we do need a kind of structural analysis which does not assume stability and continuity. In the book already quoted, Southall observes that there is still difficulty in finding the concepts for representing in structural terms the changes in African societies consequent on industrialization. Among the Kachin and Shan populations of North-East Burma, E. R. Leach was faced with a related problem in the analysis of political structure, and his way of handling it is suggestive for other studies of structural change.

His theoretical interests were aroused by the fact that the neighbouring Shans and Kachins, to all appearances very different peoples and so treated as distinct cultural and social groups in earlier writings, were in reality not so easy to sort out. He quotes for example the evidence given before a Court of Inquiry, where one man clearly considered that for seventy years all his family had been simultaneously both Shans and Kachins: 'as a Kachin the witness was a member of the Pawyam lineage of the Lahtaw(ng) clan. As a Shan he was a Buddhist and a member of the Hkam clan, the royal house of Mong Mao state.'

Persons might thus claim membership of two groups whose political structures and cultures, as they had been considered in writings upon them, were not only different but contrasting, the Shans with their feudal hierarchy, the Kachins egalitarian or anarchical. Leach saw it differently, and treats Shan and Kachin as two ideal types or models of political and social systems, not as two social groups. When they are thus seen as theoretical systems, it is possible for the anthropologist to create a model of their interaction which enables us better to understand what really happens among this population. There is a choice of alternatives, Leach finds:

In such situations as we find in the Kachin Hills area, any particular individual can be thought of as having a status position in several different social systems at the same time. To the individual himself such systems present themselves as alternatives or inconsistencies in the scheme of values by which he orders his life. The overall process of structural change comes about through the manipulation of these alternatives as a means of social advancement. Every individual in a society, each in his own interest, endeavours to exploit the situation as he perceives it, and in doing so the collectivity of individuals alters the structure of society itself.

And he further shows how ritual and myth in these circumstances provide a statement of ideal relations within the society which practice often flatly contradicts.

These are suggestions that could be followed up in the study of other communities, where what must be presumed logically, or are known historically, to have once been different and separated cultures and societies, are now politically interfused, as increasingly over much of the world. And many of the societies which had little recorded history of change a few decades ago now have much. An account of their social structures must therefore take into account that historical development, giving a fuller representation of their structure than could be obtained by study over a shorter period, and perhaps having some predictive value.

We have considered only a few of the theoretical interests of modern social anthropology, but the kind of thought here exemplified primarily in the field of politics could be matched in many others—in the study of myth and religion, in economics, kinship, language and so forth. Much quantitative material has been collected and analysed also, but to have discussed many technical aspects of anthropological research would have required a sort of book that this was not intended to be. Also, the relations of social anthropology with other studies, especially with history and sociology, are being reappraised, as it detaches itself from the biological and archaeological disciplines with which it first began. In other directions too, particularly in the combination of sociological, literary, and linguistic studies, there is much movement. The subject has been growing and changing rapidly since the second world war, and even in the last few years, and it will probably continue to do so as it continues to recruit more and more students with diverse backgrounds, who bring their own knowledge into the subject also.

When the work of many anthropologists is considered simultaneously in a general book it may appear that the ground covered is too vast for a single discipline. In practice it is not found to be so, for the organizing principles which connect this varied information are relatively few, and moreover, after laying a foundation in this general knowledge, the student tends to work mainly in a small sector of it. The anthropological view, confirmed by results, is that the depth of knowledge then acquired is proportionate to its original breadth. Social anthropology provides a kind of outline map of the social world, and in doing so has justified Tylor in his original recommendation of Anthropology to a general public:

In times when subjects of education have multiplied, it may seem at first sight a hardship to lay on the heavily pressed student a new science. But it will be found that the real effect of anthropology is rather to lighten than increase the strain of learning. In mountains we see the bearers of heavy burdens contentedly shoulder a carrying-frame besides, because they find its weight more than compensated by the convenience of holding together and balancing the load. So it is with the science of Man and Civilization, which connects in a more manageable whole the scattered subjects of an ordinary education.

Select Bibliography

Note: Since the sources of the main quotations are adequately indicated in the text, I have not listed the references separately. The following is a list of books for further reading, some of them already cited and some not.

1. INTRODUCTORY AND GENERAL

Beattie, J. H. M., 'Social Anthropology' (Article in *New Outline of Modern Knowledge*), 1956
Benedict, Ruth, *Patterns of Culture*, 1934
Emmet, D., *Function, Purpose and Powers*, 1958
Evans-Pritchard, E. E., *Social Anthropology*, 1951
  (ed.) *Institutions of Primitive Society*, 1954
  Essays in Social Anthropology, 1962
Firth, R., *Human Types* (revised edn.), 1956
  Elements of Social Organization, 1951
Frazer, Sir James, *The Golden Bough* (abridged), 1922
Gluckman, M., *Custom and Conflict in Africa*, 1955
Lowie, R. H., *History of Ethnological Theory*, 1937
Royal Anthropological Institute, *Notes and Queries in Anthropology* (6th edn.), 1951
Shapiro, H. (ed.), *Man, Culture and Society*, 1956
Tylor, E. B., *Primitive Culture*, 1871
  Anthropology, 1881

2. METHOD AND THEORY

Durkheim, E., *The Rules of Sociological Method* (trans.), 1958
Leach, E. R., *Rethinking Anthropology* 1961

Nadel, S. F., *Foundations of Social Anthropology*, 1950
   Theory of Social Structure, 1957
Parsons, T., *The Social System*, 1952
Pocock, D. F., *Social Anthropology*, 1961
Radcliffe-Brown, A. R., *Structure and Function in Primitive Society*,
   1952
   (ed. Srinivas), *Method in Social Anthropology*, 1958
Weber, M., *Theory of Social and Economic Organization* (trans.), 1947

3. POLITICS

Douglas, M., *The Lele of Kasai*, 1963
Evans-Pritchard, E. E., *The Nuer*, 1940
   The Political System of the Anuak, 1940
Fallers, L. A., *Bantu Bureaucracy*, 1956
Forest, M., and Evans-Pritchard, E. E. (eds.), *African Political
   Systems*, 1940
Leach, E. R., *Political Systems of Highland Burma*, 1954
Mair, L., *Primitive Government*, 1962
Middleton, J., and Tait, D. (eds.), *Tribes Without Rulers*, 1958
Nadel, S. F., *A Black Byzantium*, 1942
Richards, A. U. (ed.), *East African Chiefs*, 1960
Schapera, I., *Government and Politics in Tribal Societies*, 1956
Southall, A. W., *Alur Society*, 1956

4. LAW

Bohannan, P., *Justice and Judgment among the Tiv*, 1957
Durkheim, E., *The Division of Labour* (trans.), 1933
Gluckman, M., *The Judicial Process among the Barotse of Northern
   Rhodesia*, 1955
Hoebel, E. A., *The Law of Primitive Man*, 1954
Maine, H. S., *Ancient Law* (with notes by Pollock), 1906
Malinowski, B., *Crime and Custom in Savage Society*, 1926

5. ECONOMICS

Firth, R., *Primitive Economics of the New Zealand Maori*, 1929 (revised
   edn., 1959)
   Primitive Polynesian Economy, 1939
Forde, C. D., *Habitat, Economy and Society*, 1934
Herskovits, M. J., *Economic Anthropology*, 1952
Malinowski, B., *Argonauts of the Western Pacific*, 1922

Mauss, N., *The Gift* (trans. I. G. Cunnison), 1954
Winter, E. H., *Bwamba Economy*, 1956

6. KINSHIP

Barnes, J. A., *Marriage in a Changing Society* (Rhodes-Livingstone
     Institute Paper No. 20), 1951
Evans-Pritchard, E. E., *Kinship and Marriage among the Nuer*, 1951
Firth, R., *We, the Tikopia*, 1936
Fortes, M., *The Dynamics of Clanship among the Tallensi*, 1945
     The Web of Kinship among the Tallensi, 1949
Lévi-Strauss, C., *Les Structures élémentaires de la parenté*, 1949
Needham, R., *Structure and Sentiment*, 1962
Phillips, A. (ed.), *Survey of African Marriage and Family Life*, 1953
Radcliffe-Brown, A. R., *Social Organization of Australian Tribes*, 1931
     and C. Daryll Forde (eds.), *African Systems of Kinship and Marriage*,
     1950
Schapera, I., *Married Life in an African Tribe*, 1940
Smith, W. Robertson, *Kinship and Marriage in Early Arabia* (ed.
     Stanley Cook), 1903

7. RELIGION AND PHILOSOPHY

Durkheim, E., *Elementary Forms of the Religious Life* (trans. J. Swain),
     1915
Evans-Pritchard, E. E., *Witchcraft, Oracles and Magic among the
     Azande*, 1937
     Nuer Religion, 1956
Forde, C. D. (ed.), *African Worlds*, 1954
Frankfort, H., *Kingship and the Gods*, 1948
Lévy-Bruhl, L., *How Natives Think* (trans.), 1926
Lienhardt, Godfrey, *Divinity and Experience, the Religion of the Dinka*,
     1961
Macbeath, A., *Experiments in Living*, 1952
Malinowski, B., *Magic, Science and Religion*, 1948
Marett, R. R., *The Threshold of Religion*, 1909
Middleton, J., *Lugbara Religion*, 1960
     and Winter, E. (eds.), *Witchcraft and Sorcery in East Africa*, 1963
Smith, W. Robertson, *The Religion of the Semites*, 1927
Steiner, F., *Taboo*, 1956
Tempels, R. P. P., *Bantu Philosophy* (trans.), 1959

Van Gennep, A., *Les Rites de Passage* (trans.), 1960
Wilson, M., *Rituals of Kinship among the Nyakusa*, 1957

8. LINGUISTICS

Bloomfield, L., *Language*, New York, 1933
Firth, J. R., *Papers in Linguistics 1934–1951*, O.U.P., 1957
Jakobson, R., *Essais de linguistique générale*, Paris, 1963
    and Halle, M., *Fundamentals of Language* (Janua Linguarum, No. 1),
    Mouton, The Hague, 1956
Malinowski, B., *Coral Gardens and their Magic* (Volume II), London,
    1935
Sapir, E., *Language*, New York, 1939

9. SOCIAL CHANGE

Firth, R., *Social Change in Tikopia*, 1959
Hunter, M., *Reaction to Conquest*, 1936
Mair, L., *Studies in Applied Anthropology*, 1957
Malinowski, B., *The Dynamics of Culture Change*, 1945
Richards, A. I. (ed.), *Economic Development and Tribal Change*, 1953
Southall, A. (ed.), *Social Change in Modern Africa*, 1961
    and Gutkind, P. C. W., *Townsmen in the Making*, 1957
Wilson, G. and M., *The Analysis of Social Change*, 1945

REGIONAL STUDIES

1. *Europe*

Arensberg, C. M., *The Irish Countryman*, 1950
Frankenberg, R., *Village on the Border*, 1957
Kenny, M., *A Spanish Tapestry*, 1961
Pitt-Rivers, J. A., *The People of the Sierra*, 1945

2. *Africa and the Middle East*

Ammar, A., *Growing up in an Egyptian Village*, 1954
Barth, F., *Nomads of South Persia: the Basseri Tribe of the Khamseh
    Confederacy*, 1961
Busia, K. A., *The Position of the Chief in the Modern Political System of
    Ashanti*, 1951
Evans-Pritchard, E. E., *The Sanusi of Cyrenaica*, 1949
Gluckman, M., and Colson, E. (eds.), *Seven Tribes of British Central
    Africa*, 1951
Goody, J., *Death, Property and the Ancestors*, 1962

Junod, H. A., *The Life of a South African Tribe*, 1912
Kuper, H., *An African Aristocracy*, 1947
Lane, E. W., *Manners and Customs of the Modern Egyptians*, 1936
Rattray, R. S., *Ashanti*, 1923
Salim, S. M., *Marsh Dwellers of the Euphrates Delta*, 1962
Schapera, I., *A Handbook of Tswana Law*, 1955
Seligman, C. G. and B. Z., *Pagan Tribes of the Nilotic Sudan*, 1932
Seligman, C. G., *Races of Africa* (4th edn.), 1966
Stenning, D. J., *Savannah Nomads*, 1959

3. *The Americas*

Eggan, F., *Social Organization of the Western Pueblos*, 1950
   Social Anthropology of North American Tribes, 1957
Kluckhohn, C., and Leighton, D., *The Navaho*, 1941
Llewellyn, K. N., and Hoebel, E. A., *The Cheyenne Way*, 1941
Lowie, R. H., *The Crow Indians*, 1935
Parsons, E. C., *Pueblo Indian Religion*, 1939
Radin, P., *The Winnebago Tribe*, 1923
Redfield, R., *The Folk Cultures of Yucatan*, 1941
Warner, W. Lloyd, and Lunt, P. S., *The Social Life of a Modern Community*, 1941
   The Status System of a Modern Community, 1942

4. *The Far East and S.E. Asia*

Barton, R. F., *The Kalingas*, 1949
Djamour, J., *Malay Kinship and Marriage in Singapore*, 1959
Embree, J. F., *Suye Mura, A Japanese Village*, 1939
Fei, Hsaio-tung, *Peasant Life in China*, 1939
Freedman, M., *Lineage Organization in Southeastern China*, 1958
Geddes, W. R., *The Land Dyaks of Sarawak*, 1954
Geertz, H., *The Javanese Family*, 1961
Gullick, J. M., *Indigenous Political Systems of Western Malaya*, 1958
Izikowitz, K. G., *Lamet: Hill Peasants in French Indo-China*, 1951
Wilkin, G. A., *Malayan Sociology*, 1921

5. *Australia and the Pacific*

Berndt, R. M., *Djanggawul*, 1952
   and Berndt, C. H., *Aboriginal Man in Australia*, 1965
Elkin, A. P., *The Australian Aborigines*, 1948 (enlarged ed., 1964)

Fortune, R. F., *Sorcerers of Dobu*, 1932
  Manus Religion, 1935
Layard, J., *Stone Men of Malekula*, 1942
Malinowski, B., *Coral Gardens and their Magic*, 1935
Oliver, D. L., *A Solomon Island Society*, 1955
Spencer, B., and Gillen, F. J., *The Native Tribes of Central Australia*,
  1899, reprinted 1965
Strehlow, T. G. H., *Aranda Traditions*, 1947

6. *India*

Bailey, F. G., *Tribe, Caste and Nation*, 1960
Bouglé, C., *Essais sur le régime des castes*, 1908
Dubois, J. A., *Hindu Manners, Customs and Ceremonies*, 1906
Dumont, L., and Pocock, D. F., *Contributions to Indian Sociology*, 1957–
Dumont, L., *Une Sous-Caste de l'Inde du Sud: organisation sociale et
  religion des Pramallai Kallan*, 1957
Furer-Haimendorf, C. von, *The Aboriginal Tribes of Hyderabad*, 1948
Ghurye, G. S., *Caste and Class in India*, 1957
Hocart, A. M., *Caste*, 1950
Hutton, J. H., *Caste in India*, 1946
Karve, I., *Kinship Organization in India*, 1953
Marriott, McKim (ed.), *Village India*, 1955
Mayer, A., *Caste and Kinship in Central India*, 1960
Srinivas, M. N., *Marriage and Family in Mysore*, 1942
  Religion and Society among the Coorgs of South India, 1952
  (ed.), *India's Villages*, 1955
Stokes, E., *The English Utilitarians and India*, 1959

Index